MW00416747

A GIFT FOR

_____

FROM

_____

DATE

_____

# Shine
# Bright
# Anyway

# Shine Bright Anyway

## 90 Affirmations

### That Declare You Are Enough
### When the World Says You're Not

## Faith Broussard Cade

*Shine Bright Anyway*

Published by Harper Celebrate, an imprint of HarperCollins Focus LLC.

Any internet addresses (websites, blogs, etc.) in this book are offered as a resource. They are not intended in any way to be or imply an endorsement by HarperCollins Focus LLC, nor does HarperCollins Focus LLC vouch for the content of these sites for the life of this book.

ISBN 978-1-4002-4663-2 (HC)
ISBN 978-1-4002-4664-9 (Audiobook)
ISBN 978-1-4002-4667-0 (eBook)

*Printed in India*

24 25 26 27 28 MAN 5 4 3 2 1

*To my sweet Sydney.*
*You pulled me through.*
*I started writing these notes so that I could heal,*
*because I wanted to be there for you—*
*to watch you grow and bloom.*
*Being your mama inspired me to fight.*
*Many days, you were the only reason I had*
*to push through, to keep going.*
*But your perfect light illuminated my darkest*
*days, and I learned to shine because of you.*
*I learned to construct my narrative, rather than*
*blindly accepting the one being given to me.*
*Thank you for teaching me that no matter how dreary*
*my situation may be, I can still choose to shine.*
*I love you with my whole heart.*

# Contents

# Introduction

Dear friend,

Have you found yourself so deeply embedded in a cycle of self-neglect that you are often left feeling weary and utterly depleted? Are you so used to pouring into everyone else that you struggle to remember who you really are, what you're passionate about, and ultimately, how you want to experience the beautiful life you've been given?

Believe me, I've been there, and when personal tragedy overturned my life in 2018, I quickly realized I could no longer sustain the toxic level of stress and overwhelm that had been my baseline for as long as I could remember. Something had to change because the pressure to perform was destroying me. After receiving a devastating health diagnosis, I had a choice to make: Do I continue to cling to the facade of being a superhero, or do I ensure a healthy future for myself by releasing the need to control all outcomes, please everyone, and play the role that others had chosen for me?

Throughout the pages of this book, you may find that my journey to self-acceptance and appreciation is similar to yours. Maybe you feel stuck in a cycle of fear or brokenness or defeat, and you question whether you are enough. Perhaps you're tired of constantly seeking validation from others only to be left unfulfilled time and time again.

My hope is that this book will be a safe space and a respite for you, a place where you feel seen, heard, understood, and unconditionally loved and accepted. A place where you learn to honor your voice and walk in your wholeness. I hope that you embrace the brilliance that radiates from you and the strength that is within you. And that even when the world tries to diminish the magnificence of your light, you will choose to shine bright anyway.

Faith Broussard Cade

## PART ONE

# You Are
# Not
# Broken

Stop trying to "fix" yourself; you're NOT
broken! You are perfectly imperfect
and powerful beyond measure.

**—STEVE MARABOLI**

# Tell Your Story

On January 9, 2018, a tragic car accident left me with a traumatic brain injury and post-concussion syndrome, conditions from which I'm still recovering more than six years later. Conditions that shifted the trajectory of my life and my career. That prevented me from taking care of my family and holding my then-three-year-old daughter. That almost cost me my home. That caused me four-to-five-day stretches of chronic insomnia for years. Conditions so painful and consuming that they made me question my sanity, my calling, and my purpose in this world. Conditions that have, at times, convinced me that because no one else could see my struggles, maybe they weren't real.

I'm still fighting those battles every single day with intention and determination. The intention to turn my pain into purpose. The determination to help others voice their truths and refuse to suffer in silence. To advocate for themselves and what they need. My experience inspired me to view life as a no-judgment zone for myself and others. Maybe if we had more of these spaces, more of us would feel comfortable opening up about our struggles and triumphs. Maybe we would all feel just a little less alone. We would realize that our stories connect us to each other and create safe havens where we can retreat when we need the warmth of people who "just get it." Where we can be honest. Where we can feel *all* of our feelings without having to explain why we feel them.

My story came from the darkest, most desolate time of my life. And in telling my story, in sharing transparently, I have discovered that my personal healing has led to the healing of many others. For that, my heart is incredibly grateful.

Please, tell your story—whatever it is. It has a beautiful purpose to fulfill in this world.

Tell your story. The one about the thing that almost took you out. About the dark place you had to fight every second to pull yourself out of. Because that's the story that gives others the courage to share their stories. That's the story that saves lives.

# Claim Your Truth

After my accident, it took me a while to realize that no matter what I'm going through, I can choose to stand in the truth of who I am.

The truth of my hurt.

The truth of my disappointment.

The truth of my anger.

The truth of my wholeness.

And you can stand in your truth! You are not broken. You are wounded. Those two things are very different. Maybe something or someone has hurt you. That is an unfortunate and inevitable part of life. Depending upon the situation or person that caused you pain, you may feel utterly decimated, like you've been broken or crushed beyond repair.

But what happened to you *is not* who you are. That situation or person does not get to define you. Only you get to do that. You alone have that power. Claim that truth for yourself. Maybe a perspective shift is helpful here. When you are in a different place in life, how do you want to look back on this experience? Can you reflect on the pain as a necessary catalyst for the changes you needed to make in your life? Can you choose to be grateful for the resilience and wisdom you gained along your healing journey because you were forced out of your comfort zone? You have the authority to choose how you will use times of adversity in your life.

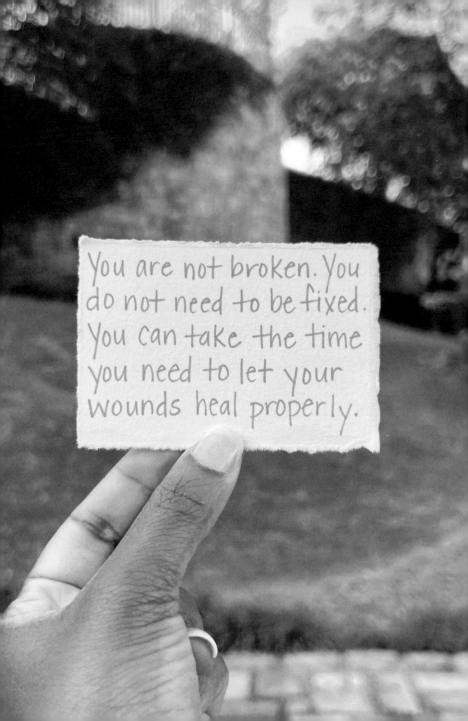

# Be Your Own Hero

There are so many days I wish to be someone else—anyone else other than myself.

The perfect mom.

The best wife.

The most effective counselor.

The most dependable friend.

The woman with the perpetually tidy house who always comes up with new recipes and never cooks the same thing twice.

I want to do things well. I want to know I am doing a good job and that what I am doing matters. That my effort makes a difference. That all the things I do for my family, my clients, and my friends have value. That the people I work so hard to take care of actually feel the impact of my actions in a meaningful way.

I am looking for them to validate the work I am doing, to affirm me and make me feel like the hero I am always trying to be. Sometimes that external validation comes, but many times it doesn't.

And when it doesn't come, then what? When no one is singing my praises and thanking me profusely, does that make my contribution any less significant? Does it negate who I am or the value of the service I shared? Of course not! Perhaps there's a desire deep inside all of us to be liked, valued, and validated. It's almost as if we look to others to confirm our "enoughness." And yet everything you and I have always looked for from other people, we already have deep inside ourselves. We are the embodiment of our wildest dreams. We have *everything* we need inside us to be the person we look up to and admire.

Use what you have. Your unique gifts and talents will not let you down. That compassionate, thoughtful, brilliant woman with a heart of gold is inside you. She's always been there. Waiting patiently for you to love and accept her for the exquisitely beautiful and phenomenal hero she is.

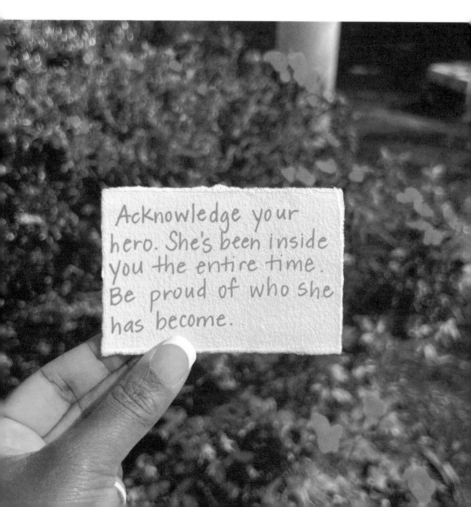

# Your Best Is Enough

Sweet friend, your best is enough.

Even if your to-do list is still full at the end of the day.

Even if your child had a meltdown on the way to school.

Even if you've reheated your coffee three times already.

Even if the laundry is overflowing, the bills need to be paid, and you forgot to thaw something to cook for dinner.

Even if you forgot to mail that out-of-town relative's birthday card.

Even if your house isn't spotless.

Even if you didn't make it to the gym today.

Even if your inner critic is relentlessly reminding you of all the broken promises you've made to yourself and all the goals you haven't yet accomplished.

Even if you can't be everything to everyone.

The bottom line is that our best is *all* we can do. We can worry and stress and wish that we could do more, but ultimately, all we can do is our best. We must learn to accept that no amount of pressure we place on ourselves can make us superhuman or extend our capacity to produce when our minds, bodies, and souls are weary. We can allow ourselves to rest in the truth that we do not have to run ourselves into the ground to prove that we are committed to our families, our jobs, our goals, or the larger world around us. Our "best" is not what we give only after we find ourselves depleted and burnt-out. Our best is what we're able to give to others and still maintain a healthy standard of care for ourselves.

Every day your best may look different, but today, your best is *enough*.

# Be Present and Engaged

Last Christmas I thought I could do it all. I shopped, baked, worked, mommed, and wifed myself into a sickbed for two weeks. I felt terrible. I missed out on so many Christmas events because I exhausted myself. Contrary to popular belief, you do not have to work yourself to the point of exhaustion. The opposite of burnout is *engagement*.

When was the last time you felt fully present and engaged in the moment without anticipating what's coming next? If you are finding yourself feeling completely detached from your daily activities and unable to experience genuine fulfillment, you may need to reduce the amount of time you spend doing things that do not bring you joy and be intentional about adding more of what you love to your life.

Some things are nonnegotiables. Others are not. Consider eliminating those joy-stealers and replacing them with things that feed your soul, nourish your spirit, and replenish what you so willingly pour out every single day. You don't have to have something on your calendar to be unavailable. Rest is a perfectly good reason. "No" is a complete sentence, no explanation necessary. It is for *you* to decide if you want to give to others from your overflow, not from your deficit, because giving from your deficit ultimately puts you at a disadvantage, draining you of the energy you were given to fulfill your purpose and change the world. The time you spend doing things you enjoy is not wasted. It is an investment in your overall well-being—*you* have to believe that the investment is worth it. *You* have to believe that you are your best self when your tank is full. *You* have to believe that being present and engaged is enough.

You do not have to work
yourself to the point of
a breakdown to prove
that you are dedicated
to your dreams. You are
most effective when
your cup is full.

# You Are Becoming

Have you ever looked at old photos of yourself and realized how unhinged you must have been back then to pick yourself apart when you were absolutely fabulous? Do you now wish you could look like *that* again?

You are not alone. What were we even thinking? After twelve years of marriage, two whole kids, and more trials and tribulations than I like to admit, my perspective on my previous self is quite different.

After the car accident, I fought my absolute hardest to recover so that I could get back to my old job, my old life, my old sense of normalcy. But when I learned to accept that my purpose in life might come in different packaging than I had planned, I opened myself to new and incredible ways that my life could impact others. Choosing to accept redirection grew my capacity for helping others beyond anything I ever could have imagined or predicted.

It's so easy to look to the past and torture ourselves by romanticizing the person we used to be. Maybe we were a few pounds lighter. Maybe we had fewer gray hairs and laugh lines. Maybe we had more free time and not as many obligations. Maybe we could leave town or meet friends for dinner at a moment's notice. Now it may take months to plan anything, and there's a good chance something will come up to cancel it anyway.

The reality of life, whether you like it or not, is that change is constant. So why not change for your benefit? Give yourself grace. Embrace the tenacity you have gained to overcome the what-ifs of the past. Trust that you are growing, you are changing, and you are becoming the most beautiful, fulfilled, and whole version of yourself. The best is yet to come.

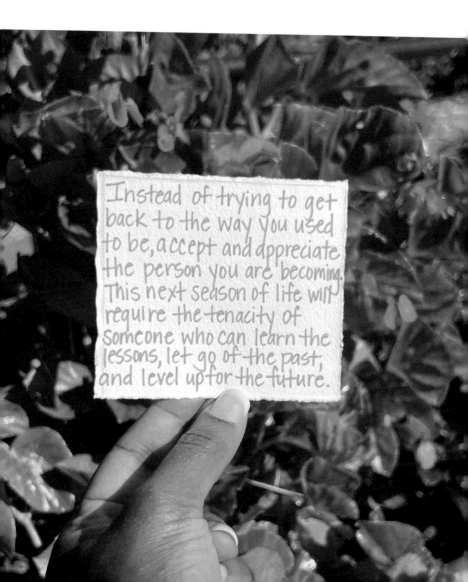

# You Are Enough

Our thoughts about our lives and the world around us eventually create the realities we experience. Take a minute. Think about it. How many negative thoughts about yourself cycle through your mind every day?

If nothing comes to mind, try this: plan to do something outside of your normal routine in the next few days. For me, that looks like spending an entire day in Barnes & Noble, wandering blissfully through the rows of books, and allowing myself to dream about taking a weeklong vacation where I do nothing but read to my heart's content. How about you? Plan to do something adventurous, exciting, or completely out of character for you. Maybe even plan to take a day off from work (gasp!) to go on your exploratory quest.

What kinds of thoughts popped into your head? Was it something like: *What in the world do I think I'm doing? I can't take a day off work! What will my boss and coworkers think? If I take a day off, I know I'm just gonna come back to double the work, and then I'll regret it. I've never been parasailing, hiking, or rock climbing before! What if I die?*

Guess what? That voice inside your head, your inner critic, is doing exactly what it's supposed to do. It's trying to keep you safe. It's warning that you could possibly put yourself in danger. Something bad could happen. And that is true. So acknowledge the caution and then make a choice about how you want to proceed.

Do you want to live a life dominated by fear, pessimism, and monotony? Or do you want to feel alive, challenged, and excited about all the adventures life has to offer? Sometimes our feelings mislead us, causing us to feel ordinary and inadequate. Every one of us is afraid of something, but we cannot allow fear to rob us of the extraordinary lives we were meant to live. Remember that you are exquisite, you are exceptional, and you are enough. Go out there and live boldly.

The mind is so powerful. What we believe is what we manifest in our lives. So believe that you are valuable and worthy and strong and loved and joyful and brave and unique and powerful beyond measure.

# You Are Not a Fraud

Why do we disqualify ourselves from being successful before we even start? Who told us to doubt our abilities and our power? What could we accomplish if we held up our heads and believed that we have everything we need inside us to succeed? The possibilities would be endless!

I often feel that because I'm so timid and introverted, I don't deserve to speak in front of audiences and share with others in such an influential way. Yet here I am, talking to large groups of women on a regular basis!

Whatever negative messages may be troubling you, stressing you, or discouraging you today, know those voices are not your own. Those are the voices of all the people who have criticized or doubted you. The people who told you that you didn't belong in the room. The people who told you that you were too loud, too opinionated, or too much. The people who *suggested* that you pursue an easier career path because you've got enough to take care of at home.

Listen to me: you deserve to be here. You deserve to explore opportunities that intrigue you. You deserve to have a life and interests outside of your home. Don't let imposter syndrome win. You are not a fraud. You know how hard you've worked and all the energy you've invested. Do not waste time worrying about the worst-case scenario. Focus your thoughts and your energy on the best possible outcome: you and your family are thriving, your mental health is flourishing, your marriage is full of love and contentment, your children are healthy and cared for, your friendships are genuine, your business is successful, and your every need is met.

   Believe it. Meditate on those things that make you smile, and fill your heart with wonder. Your life will line up with your thoughts. Make sure those thoughts are exactly what you want your life to be.

You are not a fraud. You have put in the work. Do not waste precious energy doubting your worth or capabilities. You deserve to be here.

# The Answer Is No

Are you feeling pressure to be someone or something? Or, more likely, to be *everything* to *everyone*? I know I do. And when you don't measure up or get it all done or make everyone happy or lose your temper, do you feel as if you're not enough? Believe me, I struggle with this too, but I'm working on it.

Being a people pleaser is exhausting work. It zaps our time and energy. It uses guilt to shame us into taking on more than we can or want to. It reinforces the lie that we will hurt, disappoint, or upset others if we say no. It tells us that we will do irreparable damage to our friendships if we set boundaries and choose not to attend the next cookout, girls' trip, birthday party, or game night.

But we can refute the lies that our guilt tells us. We can trust ourselves and our intuition. We can listen to our minds and bodies and opt out of things that will stretch us beyond our capacity in an unhealthy way. Repeat after me:

- *No.* I don't have to go along when I don't feel like it.
- *No.* I will not let folks guilt me into going where I don't want to go.
- *No.* I will not let others convince me that I am a bad friend or person when I honor my boundaries.

Now that *that's* out of the way, relax and do whatever it is you want to do with your free time today. You deserve it.

# Show Up

Several years ago, I wanted to stop showing up. The pain of recovering from an invisible disability felt like a hurdle I'd never be able to get over. I made the mistake of letting those feelings of discouragement linger far too long and delay my healing journey. But once I started to write daily positive affirmations to myself and share my notes online, I realized that I can't *not* show up. I can't *not* do this work. This work heals and changes lives. I don't want to choose to not show up for myself and for others. And quite honestly, having a reason to show up has changed my life—because it saved my life.

Nothing good or constructive can come from replaying the guilt of our past mistakes or trauma. So you made a mistake. We all do. At the time you thought it was the right decision, but it didn't work out. You made the best decision you could with the information you had. Fine. Refocus, regroup, and figure out your next move. Forgive yourself for the choices you made when you didn't know any better. There is grace and redemption in moving on.

What you practice is what you become. Rehearsing your short-comings only ensures that you keep playing the same role. Eventually, the discouragement and negative self-talk will convince you that it's not even worth trying anymore. You start rationalizing why you should even continue showing up.

Find your reason to show up. Make your first appearance *today*. One day you will become the person you've always wanted to be. You have everything you've ever needed inside you just waiting for you to ditch the facades, the pretenses, and the masks. Commit today to uncover your reason, to appreciate it, and to *live boldly in it*. You'll be so happy you did.

Your messy spaces do not disqualify you. They merely highlight the places where you are growing, changing, and evolving into the best version of yourself.

# Move On

Every single person in your life, whether permanent or temporary, is there for a reason. To teach you about love, pain, your own strength, forgiveness, loyalty, growth, relationships, and compassion. It is necessary to learn the lessons they bring.

One hard lesson I've learned over the past several years is that I cannot expect others to hold the same views and values I do about relationships. I cannot expect that everyone will feel the way I feel, love the way I love, or care the way I care. That is okay. We are all inherently different, and we cannot control anyone but ourselves. But what I can do, what I can control, is how I allow those people to occupy space in my life, if at all. You have the power to do the same. That is how you protect your mind, your joy, and your peace.

Be watchful. Be observant. Be wise.

When someone wants the best for you, their excitement will be evident. When they don't, they'll seem uninterested or try to diminish your excitement about it.

Protect *your* dream.

Stop maintaining one-sided friendships out of obligation. We all know the "friend" who checks in just to make sure she's still doing better than you are. Just because you've known her for years doesn't mean she's supposed to be a part of your life forever. And it also doesn't make her a bad person. It just may be time for you to move on.

Not everyone wants the best for you, and accepting that can

be both hurtful and disappointing. Reevaluate your circle. Protect your space. Reclaim your inner tranquility. It's not mean or rude; it's necessary.

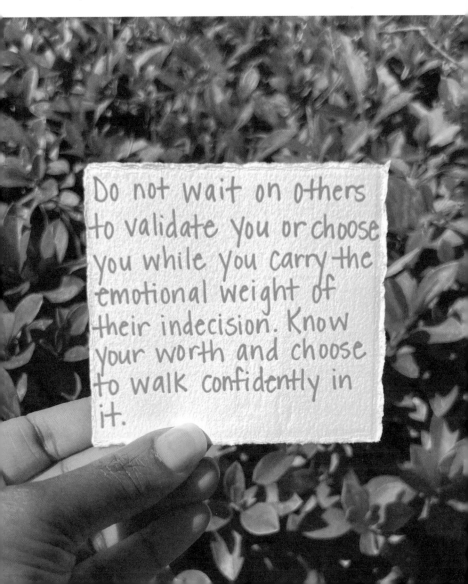

Do not wait on others to validate you or choose you while you carry the emotional weight of their indecision. Know your worth and choose to walk confidently in it.

# From Pain to Purpose

Working through the daily challenges of my traumatic brain injury is something I never planned to share. It is personal and hard and invisible to the outside world. So I kept that struggle to myself for a long time. Until I decided I needed accountability in caring for myself if I was going to live a full life again. I realized that maybe someone else out there was struggling with an unseen condition and needed to know they are not alone. Your story of overcoming is not just for you.

Yeah, maybe someone else could have gone through a similar situation. Maybe they could have survived something worse than you did. But not everyone could have done it with the same amount of grit, strength, or grace, with their faith, sanity, and will to live still intact. Not everyone could do it without allowing bitterness and resentment to consume them. Not everyone could do it without becoming mad at the world. Not everyone could do it and still have the courage to love, trust, and try again.

With everything going on in the world today, many of us are one traumatic experience, one toxic interaction, one abusive touch, one toddler meltdown, one past-due bill, one inconsiderate work deadline, one family argument, one sink of dirty dishes, or one sleepless night away from a mental health crisis. It could be any one of us. Not one of us is immune to the damaging effects of environmental stressors on our mental health.

Today, practice empathy and compassion. They make the world we live in just a little more bearable, especially if you're struggling to hold on. You were given your mountain to climb and conquer, which in turn gives others the strength to endure the scrapes, scars, and bruises of their own climb. Because one day, they, too, will see that all the *pain* led them to their *purpose*.

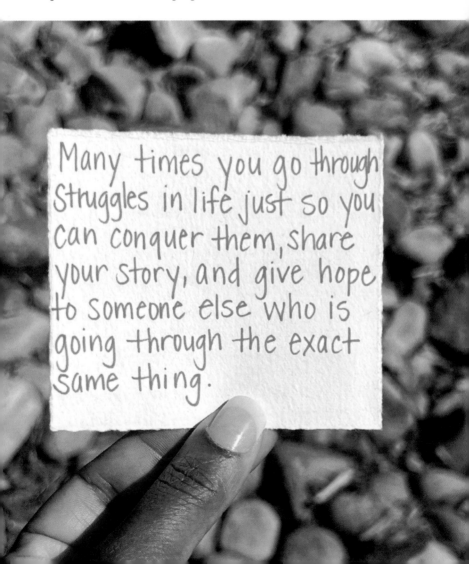

Many times you go through struggles in life just so you can conquer them, share your story, and give hope to someone else who is going through the exact same thing.

# It's Okay to Not Be Okay

It took several years of striving for perfection and being disappointed in myself to realize that I can still be okay even if my life isn't flawless. I am okay even if I had trouble focusing today, lost track of time, and had to order takeout for dinner. It's okay to not be okay. It's not a complaint to admit that.

Not everything in life will go according to your plans. You are allowed to feel disappointed. *And* you are allowed to move through the discomfort of that space. You are allowed to continue to be hopeful and optimistic because you trust things won't be this way forever.

I'm the author of my narrative. I hold the pen. Just as you're the author of your narrative. You hold the pen. What story will your narrative tell? The story of your inner critic and the naysayers? Or the story of your self-compassion and resilience?

You have the authority to rewrite the story you keep telling yourself about who you are. You may not be perfect, but every day you are doing your best to love who you are while evolving into the person you want to become. Embrace *that* narrative. You've earned it.

Think about it this way: you have the power to build up or tear down your own house.

Examine your thoughts, words, actions, eye rolls, lip smacks, and tone of voice. Are you tearing down or lifting up the people around you? No one wants to walk on eggshells all the time. You help set the tone in your environment. Make sure it's one that is healthy and wholesome.

You don't have to pretend to be okay. Your strength isn't in denying that you feel hurt. Strong people cry all the time. Your strength lies in your determination to get up and get through. To survive. And to come out on the other side ready to live by the lessons you've learned.

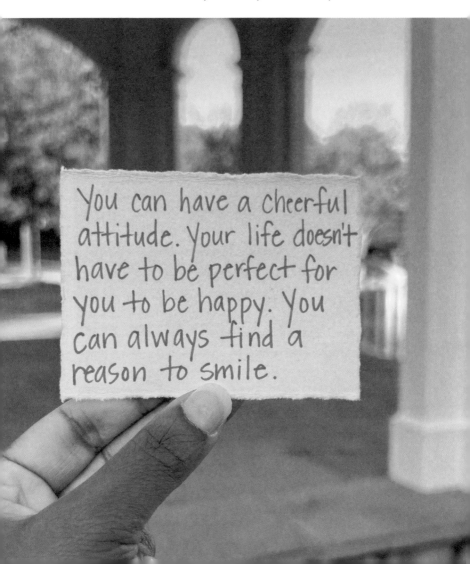

# You Are Not Broken

Feeling overwhelmed? Of course you are! I am! Look at the number of things on our plates. I have a family who wants to spend time with me, clients who expect a focused counselor, a house to clean, homework to oversee, friends who deserve more than sporadic texts, and a refrigerator that refuses to stock itself. We say we're "tired," but is that the whole truth? Of course not! "Tired" is the easy answer. "Tired" is the simple answer. "Tired" is the palatable, socially acceptable answer that everyone will understand, nod and sigh in agreement with, and not ask any further questions about. But it doesn't even begin to describe the way we're really feeling these days.

We are human beings experiencing many of the same struggles and having the same challenges. Let's be transparent about that. Let's share our stories so that we don't feel alone. So that we can support each other and create safe spaces and communities where we can be vulnerable with each other. Let's take off the superhero cape and just be human.

Sometimes, self-care looks like taking time to nurture your goals and passions without comparing them to anyone else's. Don't downplay your accomplishments because they look different than someone else's.

Can't run a 5K? At least you made it to the gym three times this week. Didn't get to go shopping this weekend? Don't forget: you were able to pay all your bills this month. Didn't get all the laundry done? But you cooked for your family, and your kids are still alive. Didn't start that blog or online boutique like you planned to this week? You *did* get your logo finished and your business cards printed. Didn't win the Superwoman Award this week? (By the way, there is no such thing!) But you tried your best, you took deep breaths, and you didn't take your frustrations out on innocent people. Give yourself some credit.

You are winning. And that is worth celebrating!

Be gentle with yourself. The level of perfection you're trying to achieve is unrealistic and unhealthy. Adjust your expectations and allow yourself to be proud of what you have accomplished.

# Focus

If you have trouble concentrating and staying on task, you are not alone. I was diagnosed with adult ADHD at thirty-one years old and with a traumatic brain injury at thirty-three. For as long as I can remember, I have struggled with staying focused. But because I thought my inattention was my fault, I didn't ask for help—I just worked harder. I pulled all-nighters and skipped social events in college to live in the twenty-four-hour library on campus. I figured I just wasn't as smart as everyone else because they didn't spend half as much time on schoolwork as I did.

Once I completed college and graduate school and began my career as a school counselor, I thought I would be fine. I had only one job to focus on rather than multiple classes and a work-study job.

Well, I was wrong. I had so many different responsibilities, I felt like I was flailing all over the place. I felt shame and fear that I would be found out; it was only a matter of time before someone discovered how much time it took me to get myself back on task every day. I put even more pressure on myself, made more lists, and tried to predict and prevent all the ways I could possibly mess up.

It took lots of soul-searching and years of consistent therapy to adopt the mantra, "Focus on one thing at a time." Have you experienced something similar?

You have what you need to get through this situation *today*. And tomorrow, you'll have what you need to get through tomorrow. The present moment is where you're needed. Keeping yourself engaged in the moment is going to take patience and love and a lot of positive redirection. Focus on now and encourage yourself with tenderness and grace.

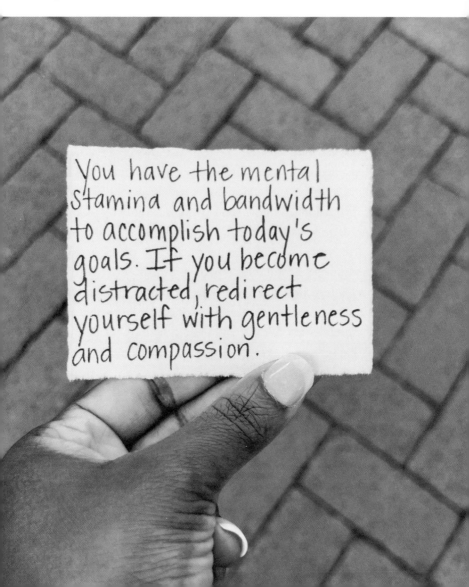

You have the mental stamina and bandwidth to accomplish today's goals. If you become distracted, redirect yourself with gentleness and compassion.

# Accept the Help

It can be extremely uncomfortable to let people in. To let them see *you*. To not be the strong one all the time. To let them pour into you the way you pour into everyone else. When you've always been the strong one, it can feel awkward and downright embarrassing to allow anyone to see that you need closeness and consideration as well. I know it was for me.

As a mental health professional, I had always been the friend people consulted for advice. So when I needed a shoulder to cry on, I suffered in silence because I didn't want people to question the legitimacy of my position. I didn't want them to assume I was incapable of helping them because I struggled with my own stuff. But when we push past the discomfort of asking for help, stop telling people we're "fine," and accept the kindness others are eager to offer us, our lives change. Our load becomes lighter. We learn how to smile and have fun again, how to be vulnerable and let the tears fall without fear of backlash or retaliation. We learn to live our truths in plain sight. And we learn that some of life's most precious blessings come to us through the hands and hearts of others.

Identify who your people are, and then cultivate the relationships necessary to contribute to your support system. Tell them what you need, and allow them to show up for you without feeling the need to control how they do so. Don't be afraid to admit that you are struggling.

When you are struggling, automate what you can. Have groceries and supplies delivered, and delegate household tasks and chores when people ask how they can help. Make a list of your people. Schedule regular check-ins. Accept their help. Then shoot them a text sometime within the next week to let them know how much you value their presence in your life. Help is a beautiful thing. Allow yourself to ask for and receive it.

# Comparison

Dear friend, repeat after me: "Celebrating someone else's success doesn't make me any less successful. There is more than enough sun for everyone."

In today's world, we have to make a deliberate choice to resist a culture of comparison. It's easier than ever to peek into other people's homes, families, and even vacations. It's also very tempting to compare the entirety of our lives with the snapshots others allow us to see of their own.

As a person who has challenges with attention and staying on task, I am aware that the quickest way for me to get distracted from what I'm supposed to be doing is to check social media. I can be super productive, catching up on emails and getting my calendar set up for the day. Then my phone lights up with a notification, and the next thing I know, I'm scrolling mindlessly through my Instagram feed comparing my life to what I see there.

Do you want to know the best way to miss out on all your blessings? By comparing your life's journey to someone else's! By using social media to check up on other people, to see how you measure up to them. By being in an imaginary competition with someone who isn't even aware there's a race going on. You have no idea what really goes on in their houses, yet you're walking around feeling as though they're outdoing you. Don't be so distracted by other people's blessings that you overlook your own.

Blessings are unique and individualized; they don't all look the same. But don't dismiss your gifts and talents because they don't resemble someone else's. Don't stop pursuing your gift because it isn't yielding immediate results. When we put all our gifts together to embrace a perspective of collaboration over competition, that mindset unifies us and strengthens our communities.

Do not compare your life or accomplishments to anyone else's. You can celebrate the success of others and appreciate your own blessings simultaneously.

# Push On

Life isn't going to be tidy and affirming all the time. You won't have an audience cheering and throwing confetti every time you do something notable or helpful. Your friends won't always see and understand your vision. Well-meaning family members may remind you repeatedly of the risk you're taking. They want the best for you and don't want to see you hurt or disappointed. That doesn't mean you should internalize their fears. Acknowledge the advice, adjust if you need to, and then push on.

Adulting can be messy. Marriage can be messy. Friendships can be messy. Parenting can be messy. Kids are almost *always* messy. So? Sometimes life is messy and unpredictable. There will be ugly cries, swollen eyes, snotty noses, and days you're sobbing so hard you can barely breathe—or maybe that's just me. But that doesn't mean you should just give up, throw in the towel, and settle for the predictable, unfulfilling life you've been trying to trick yourself into believing you're satisfied with. You do not have to do what you've always done, be what you've always been, or continue to accept what you've always accepted.

Oh, you'll definitely feel isolated and a little deranged at some point in the process of following your vision, but you're in great company. What if you don't feel ready? If you have something that sets your soul on fire with excitement and unrelenting passion, go ahead, create it, and put it out there! Why? Because the truth is that you'll probably never feel completely ready. If you look hard enough for an excuse, believe me you'll find one. (I've done the legwork, friend.)

Your life's journey is yours to shape and no one else's. No one knows what works for you better than you do. So push on past the uncertainty, and take a chance on yourself. You are worth the risk.

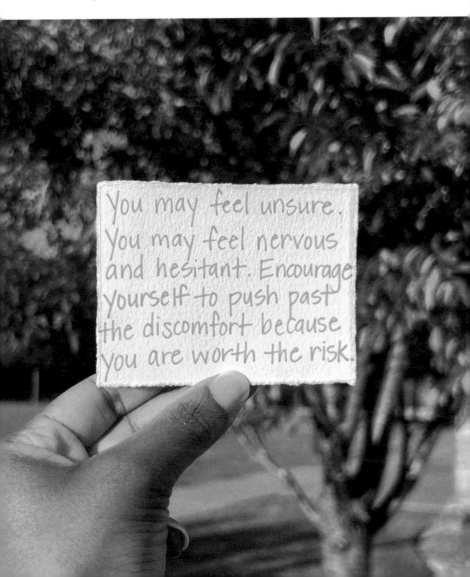

You may feel unsure. You may feel nervous and hesitant. Encourage yourself to push past the discomfort because you are worth the risk.

# Your Own Happiness

Ultimately, we are responsible for our own happiness. It is not the job of the people we love to make us happy, nor is it our job to make them happy. Many times, we put unrealistic expectations on ourselves or others and then wallow in disappointment when either they or we fail to live up to said expectations.

When I'm feeling especially irritated with everyone in my house, most of the time it isn't because they are all inconsiderate human beings who take me for granted. It's usually because I have chosen to insert myself into a situation that would be completely fine without me, often sacrificing the self-care time I had been looking forward to.

Case in point: when my sweet husband mentioned we hadn't had jambalaya for dinner in a while, my internal "good wife" antennae shot up, and the mental downward spiral began. *Did he say that because he wants me to make jambalaya for dinner tonight? I was looking forward to some self-care time! Am I being selfish for choosing not to do something thoughtful for him? It's fine. I can schedule some time for myself another day . . .*

So I gave up my *precious* alone time to make jambalaya. And for the rest of the evening, I was snippety. Ooh, I was *hot*, y'all! The sound of him breathing annoyed me because he did not acknowledge—with bells and whistles—the sacrifice I made. I became unpleasant to be around because *I* chose to give up something *I* desperately needed. I wanted everyone to compensate me for the choice *I* made *voluntarily*.

Moral of the story: keep your promise to yourself when you plan self-care. Let them eat leftovers. Or cereal. Make the jambalaya another day. They will be fine.

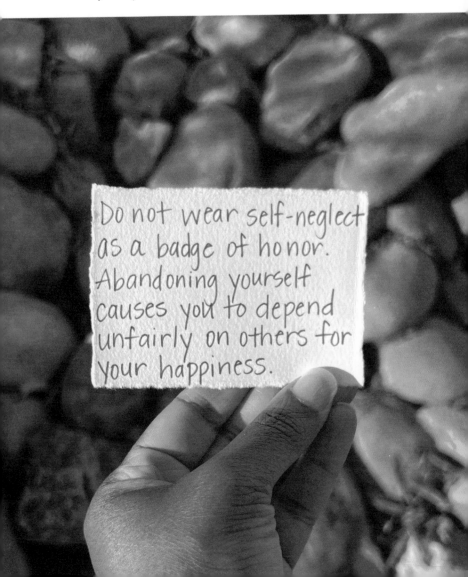

Do not wear self-neglect as a badge of honor. Abandoning yourself causes you to depend unfairly on others for your happiness.

# An Abundance of Joy

I grew up with a fear of abundance. Not because abundance in and of itself is bad, but because abundance held a connotation of gluttony and excess and selfishness. So many of us believe we should have just enough of something or maybe even a little less than the desired amount, but never a plethora of something. It's okay to have just enough money, happiness, love, friendship, food, resources, clothes, or shoes—but not too much.

For many of us, no matter how hard we work, we harbor feelings of shame around having plenty. We exhaust ourselves, working to acquire the resources that will give us margin in our busy schedules so we can actually enjoy the fruits of our labor and spend quality time with the people we love. We can afford it, but we are mortified to hire someone to clean our house once a month because what would our mothers say? We should be at least a little bit miserable about something for good measure, right? It keeps you humble.

But here is a reality check. There is no award for having too little or being the most unhappy person. You will not get a pat on the back for denying yourself joy. So embrace it. Buy an extra bag of your favorite flavor of popcorn and stash it in your bedside table so you don't have to share. Hire the housekeeper. Have fun. Abundance is not something to avoid—particularly if it is an abundance of joy.

An abundance of joy is always available to you if you are willing to discover it. You no longer have to accept lack or a scarcity mindset.

# Do Not Minimize Yourself

Playing small so other folks can feel comfortable about their mediocrity, lack of drive, and poor work ethic—*nope*, not anymore. For years, I would shrink from recognition or downplay my skills to avoid being perceived as an overachiever. I didn't want people to see me as someone who thought she was better than anyone else.

Many of us downplay our accomplishments so that it will hurt less when someone else minimizes our achievements. That is a trauma response, not a coping skill. So let's stop doing that.

Maybe someone told you that being proud of yourself was bad. Maybe they equated being proud of yourself with being prideful or thinking yourself better than others. Or perhaps they told you to appear shy and hesitant when you receive compliments, that making light of your incredible talent was synonymous with being humble.

If they did, they deceived you, and you can tell them I said so.

Peel back all the layers of the woman you thought you were supposed to be. The way you were told you were supposed to behave in order to be deemed acceptable. You will find that the woman you are meant to be has been there all along. Inside you. At your core. Waiting for you to acknowledge her existence, accept her, and love her exactly as she is.

No matter how outgoing or reserved your personality is. No matter how many times you've allowed this world to place unrealistic expectations on you or put you in a box, or made you choose to put the wants and needs of others over your own. No matter how many times you have looked to others to validate the pure magic that exists inside you.

Do not minimize yourself, friend. Putting others first and caring for their needs does not mean you are less. It means you think of yourself less, not less of yourself. You are still fabulous—more fabulous because you're using the best parts of you to serve others.

You can be humble without playing small or minimizing who you are and what you do well.

# Know Yourself

I can admit it—I'm a planner. A hard-core, color-coding, highlighters-and-matching-stickers, bookmarking type of planner. I'm the one sitting at my computer, excitedly anticipating the launch day of the newest Simplified Planner by Emily Ley so I can make my purchase and give a sigh of relief that my future is secure. Do not ask me to make plans if I don't have my planner with me. I'll just have to get back to you.

I mark my planner pages with colored dots and make a key to show what each dot represents in my life: PERSONAL, KIDS, COUNSELING, CONTENT, MEETINGS, SPEAKING ENGAGEMENTS.

It's a little intense, but it's how I'm able to get things done with multiple jobs and being responsible for two little humans.

It's taken me a while, but I've come to accept the constraints of my condition and learned to work within them instead of struggling against them. What works for other people may not work for me, and that is okay. Other people may not understand why you do things the way you do them, and they don't have to. What works best for you and your lifestyle is your decision to make.

You are the foremost expert on your life. Trust yourself to know what you need. If you are a planner, plan. If going with the flow works for you and your family, then flow. Having loved ones who can speak into your life is invaluable. But only you can know what is truly right for you.

You are the subject-
matter expert on your
life. Trust that you
are capable of making
decisions and implementing
systems that work best
for you and your family.

# Rewrite Your Story

Several months after my accident, I came to the realization that it was time to rewrite my story. I was over being a victim who let life happen to her. I decided to believe that I had a purpose, value, and a life worth living to the fullest. And you can do the same, friend. Rewrite the story you keep telling yourself about who you are. You may not be perfect, but every day you are doing your best to love who you are while evolving into the person you want to become. Embrace *that* narrative.

Grab a journal, a notebook, or a writing app and start physically writing a new story.

What would a new story look like for you? If you think you are a failure, write something like, "I am a person whose existence is essential and appreciated. I am worthy of love and respect just as I am." If you think you are not enough, perhaps write, "I am amazing just as I am. If I am not enough or too much for certain people, I give myself permission to put space between us." If you think you are too needy, try writing, "I need people in my life, but I will respect their boundaries and seek peace within myself." If you think you are too controlling, maybe jot down, "I will give people the space to be true to themselves and try doing things the way they believe is best."

Rewriting your story begins with being willing to reframe your perspective. Open your mind and heart to the possibility that you are capable of surpassing the limitations you or others have placed on you. Shift your mindset to consider all the goodness and contentment you could experience if you choose to believe in yourself. When you have reframed your thinking, revisit the pages often. Update as needed. Learn and trust that your story is needed and valuable.

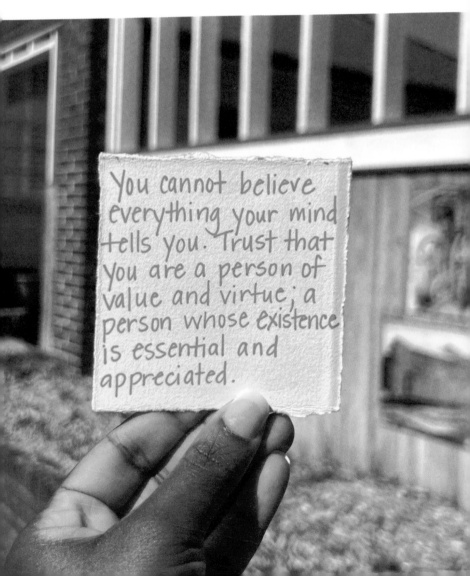

You cannot believe everything your mind tells you. Trust that you are a person of value and virtue; a person whose existence is essential and appreciated.

# Embrace Abundance

Many of us grew up hearing things like: "Don't ask for too much"; "Don't be greedy"; "Don't be ungrateful"; "Somebody else would switch places with you in a heartbeat"; "The little bit you think you have is still more than someone else has."

From comments like these, we learned to exist but not take up too much space. To not be an inconvenience or burden for anyone who was nice enough to do something for us or take care of us. We learned not to make anyone's life harder than it already was.

We then became adults who are always on time or early, never miss deadlines, overachieve, are perfectionists, avoid risks, are people-pleasers and peacekeepers, and are the nice ones—too nice, actually.

Often we end up doing everything to someone else's standards, absorbing their convictions and beliefs about life and leaving no space for self-discovery.

We've made ourselves satisfied with the least bit possible. We've convinced ourselves to settle for the crumbs that people chose to give us because at least they offered us something. And when we find people who want to love us wholly and completely, we struggle to receive their generous offering because we don't want them to regret it or realize we were never worth the sacrifice.

You don't have to settle for scraps. You can have abundance. You are worthy of relationships that overflow with loyalty, generosity, and empathy. You deserve to be wrapped up in a beautiful and lavish love that provides safety and security. You can expect rich and wonderful opportunities to become available for you. Leave the past behind. Embrace a hopeful, abundant future.

# Good Enough

Fear is the root of most people's perfectionism. There's a fear of:

- Permanence
- Moving on to start something new
- What you've done being insufficient
- Criticism
- Disapproval

- The responsibility that comes with creating and sharing what you've created
- Your work being bad
- Your work being good
- Letting go
- Losing control

The fear I struggle with the most is creating and sharing something that might draw negative criticism from others. I tend to overthink my work and try to anticipate everything someone could find wrong with it. It is exhausting.

Do not allow perfectionism to hinder your progress. Although it may give you hives to walk away from something without finishing it, I've found value in taking a break and coming back to it at a later time. Try it. Your standards for yourself are almost always much higher than what anyone else expects of you. Oftentimes what you have completed is more than enough, but you convince yourself that it is subpar because of those fears.

Do not allow fear to define you. You are so much more than that person. You can be the person who acknowledges the fear but keeps going. Who controls herself, not others. Who is learning that sometimes good enough really is good enough for right now. Perhaps your overworked and overstimulated brain needs some time to recover and replenish all that it has poured out. Just like your muscles need rest and a good soak after a grueling workout, your mind needs to recuperate as well. Giving yourself time away from a project can allow space for new and innovative ideas to form. So push past that fear of "messing up." Push past the perfectionism, and do what you can with what you have.

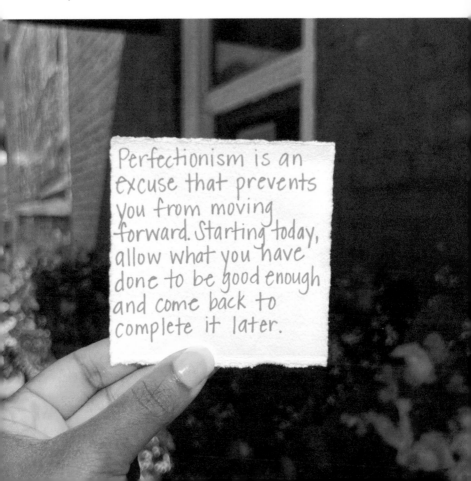

Perfectionism is an excuse that prevents you from moving forward. Starting today, allow what you have done to be good enough and come back to complete it later.

# Adjustments

I must be willing to take full responsibility for the things I've done that are holding me back. I can't continue to blame others for my lack of progress. When I make excuses to justify why I procrastinate or refuse to move forward with a project, I must accept that I made the choice to turn down an opportunity that could have been great for me.

Personal responsibility is hard. Admitting that you have been a perpetrator of self-sabotage in your life is a hard pill to swallow. Holding yourself accountable for the choices you've made that have impacted you in a negative way can be painful. Because when you do, the ball is in your court. You don't get to blame anyone else for your unhappiness or expect them to fix you.

You have to do the work. You have to be transparent with the person in the mirror and figure out what you're going to do differently. Which habits you're willing to eliminate. The negative self-talk you've allowed to plant seeds of doubt about your capabilities in your mind. The lies people have told you about yourself that you've chosen to believe, oftentimes subconsciously.

You *can* make adjustments. All hope is not lost. The first step is being honest with yourself about what is not working. Are you repeating destructive behaviors yet expecting a different result? Do you give up on something at the first sight of difficulty? Deep down inside, are you afraid that you have the capability to do something great, but it would require you to come out of hiding and allow others to really see you? You have the power to change that. Start today by committing to embrace every part of who you are. The good and the not so good. And decide that you are going to do the work it takes to be the best version of yourself.

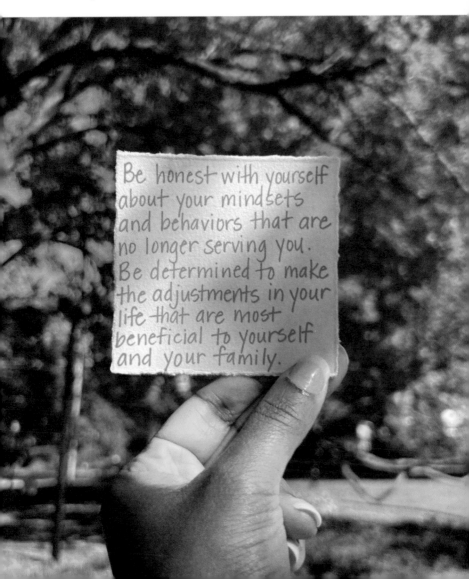

Be honest with yourself about your mindsets and behaviors that are no longer serving you. Be determined to make the adjustments in your life that are most beneficial to yourself and your family.

# Be Courageous

When I'm hesitant to start something, it's usually because I'm looking into the distant future and worrying about having what I need to see the project through to completion.

I've always had a passion for helping others, which is why I became a counselor. After the car accident and having to leave my job, I wasn't sure how to continue helping even though I knew it was what I was meant to do. During my recovery, I reevaluated my role as a mother, and the light finally switched on for me. I felt like I was the only one struggling to be everything my family needed while also making time to heal and take care of myself. As women we do so much for others that we often feel guilty prioritizing our self-care and personal wellness.

We need a safe space to live out the full, uncensored truths of who we are. Seeing that need gave me the courage to create a platform of support for women. I've been unsure and scared and embarrassed and ready to give up. Why? Because, like many others, I struggle with feelings of self-doubt. We don't trust ourselves, we look for outside validation, we don't believe in our abilities, or we procrastinate, hoping the nudge we feel to do something will pass so we don't have to act on it. But what if we pushed through the initial scary feelings of discomfort? Maybe then we'd have the opportunity to watch things work in our favor.

What keeps you from finishing things? Do you get paralyzed by worry? Do you find it hard to get organized? Are you scared of moving forward? Are you easily distracted? Push past the discomfort. Stop thinking up what-ifs. Be courageous and take one step in the direction of your future.

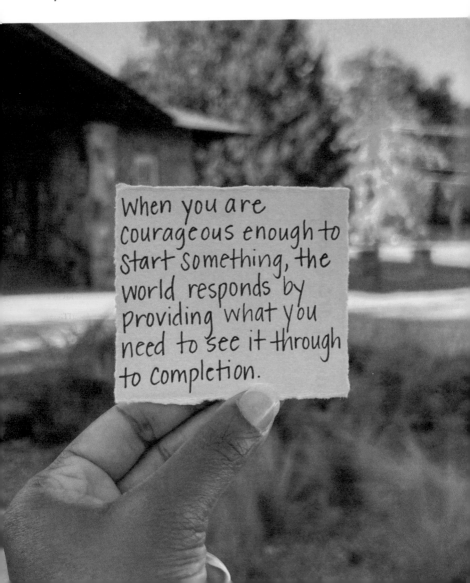

When you are courageous enough to start something, the world responds by providing what you need to see it through to completion.

# Patience

I'm guilty of wanting to be *there* already.

As soon as I start something, I want to be great at it. I'm going to follow the rules, and if I follow the rules, then whatever I'm doing should turn out perfectly. I'm not a slacker, so I know I'm going to give it my best effort. I'll probably give it 110 percent and still find a way to go back and give it a little more. And because I have a stellar work ethic, surely I should be guaranteed the most desirable outcome, right?

It doesn't always work that way. Unfortunately, some habits are hard to break, and some new behaviors aren't so easily incorporated into our lives—even if we are geniuses or overachievers. Maybe we were raised in an environment where we saw our mothers and grand-mothers work themselves to the point of burnout to take care of everyone else. Maybe we interpreted that as the best way to be a wife and mother, and so we became a part of a self-neglect cycle. But when we decide this isn't a cycle we want to perpetuate, that doesn't mean we're going to wake up tomorrow and know exactly how to make time for ourselves, set healthy boundaries, stop people-pleasing, and prioritize our mental and emotional health.

Breaking a bad habit and learning a new skill is not easy. Commit to the process. Have patience. A new skill takes practice. There is no shortcut to achieve the life skills you need. Just keep trying. The journey may not look the way you thought it would, but don't give up. Surround yourself with people who support your decision to improve your life. You can do it.

# Work in Progress

When you make the decision to change, more than likely there will be someone who reminds you of who you used to be. They may even doubt your ability to make those changes permanent. When I began to listen to what my body and mind needed, I realized I had to start with setting healthy boundaries. Some people in my life were quite resistant to that shift, and even though I knew enforcing those boundaries was best for me, I was tempted to let outside voices divert the course of my growth journey.

Your evolution becomes less about doing what is best for you and more about determining whether you can do this without failing miserably and making a fool of yourself. And maybe you begin to question whether you should even try. There is a certain amount of safety and comfort that comes with settling into the role people have always expected you to fill. Doing what people expect of you keeps them satisfied and out of your hair. They don't ask uncomfortable questions, and you don't have to come up with answers. Everyone is happy . . . but you.

Going along to get along can make you feel silenced and constrained. You feel you've outgrown where you are, and you need to get up and stretch your legs. You've become bored and spiritless; you're going through the motions. There is a hunger deep inside you to emerge from the box where you've been confined and actually live. You're doing the inner work, and a new version of you is ready to break free. Remember, you are a work in progress. Change is not instant. But it is worth it.

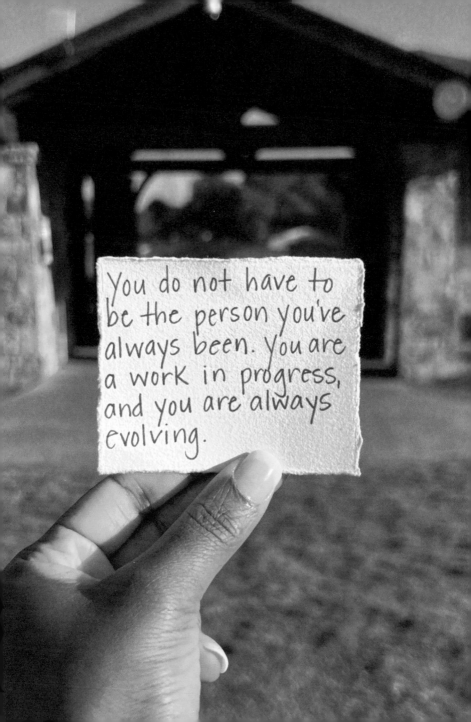

# You Made It

You. Made. It. You made it through:

- All the days you thought were too hard
- All the moments you thought were too painful
- All the situations and circumstances and challenges you thought would break you
- The heartbreak and betrayal from people you trusted

The feelings of paralyzing self-doubt and "not-enoughness" that threaten to discourage you from chasing your dreams and pursuing your purpose, they're just feelings. Oh sure, there have been (and will be in the future) plenty of days when you're ready to throw in the towel. There will be hard days when things go wrong, when your patience is *very* thin, when your faith is tested, and your heart feels heavy. There will be days when you feel that no one could possibly understand the things you struggle with or how weak and inadequate you feel. You'll wonder how you'll ever muster up the strength and courage to put one foot in front of the other and not burst into tears or crumble under the weight of everything you're carrying. But you won't give up. I believe in you. You're a survivor.

You took breaks when you needed to, but you didn't stop showing up for yourself and the people you love. You acknowledged the hurt, allowed yourself to feel your feelings, and chose to persevere. You chose to be the author of your own story and refused to be manipulated into believing you are alone. You reached out for help and accepted it with grace and gratitude. You prioritized your mental health and let some things go. Give yourself credit for that, and celebrate the incredible strength and determination inside you. You deserve it.

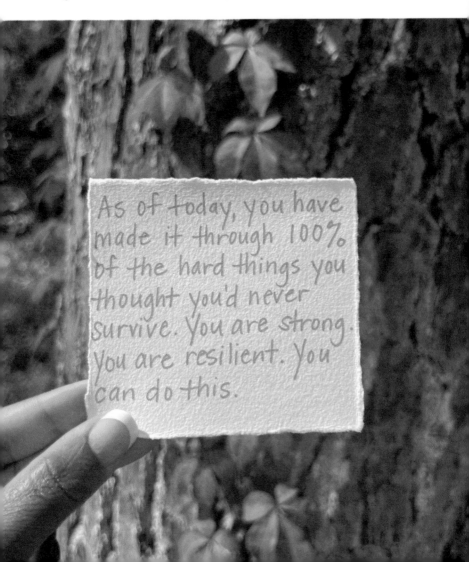

❀

# PART TWO

# Take Care of Yourself

❀

Self-care is one of the active ways that I love myself. When you can and as you can, in ways that feel loving, make time and space for yourself.

—TRACEE ELLIS ROSS

# Healing Path

I haven't been the same since 2018 when I was in the car accident. It's been superhard to accept and to share with the world. But, I've been honest and transparent.

I've struggled with chronic pain and headaches, memory loss, difficulty concentrating, and unshakable anxiety. Amid all of the physical, mental, and emotional challenges I was facing on a daily basis, I lost my job as a school counselor, which caused an unimaginable financial strain on our little family. The amount of stress we were under felt unfair and oftentimes unbearable. I struggled to maintain a sense of normalcy for my family—to be the wife and mother I'd always been—while also focusing on my own recovery. I felt like I couldn't regain a sense of control, no matter how hard I tried.

But I knew I had to find a way to prioritize my mental health. So I began a little self-love challenge: I committed to nourishing my heart and mind by writing a positive affirmation to encourage myself no matter what that day would bring. I decided to take just five minutes each day to write a note that I'd post on Instagram for accountability. My intention was to write them for fifteen days, and here I am, more than six years later, still writing those notes. Not just for me, but also for you.

This is the personal healing path that was intended for me. Writing affirmations works for me. Sharing those words of reassurance with the world breathed life into parts of me that had been suffocated by trauma, shame, and self-doubt. You have the same power to determine what your path to restoration looks like.

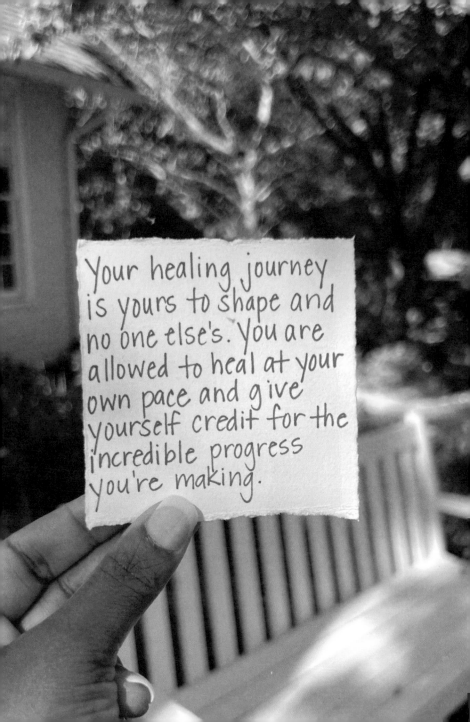

# Self-Care

We've gotten so used to looking like we're holding it all together that we're afraid to admit we're falling apart in more ways than one. It's as if we're the only ones struggling and everyone else has life completely figured out. We're terrified to admit we're tired of doing, tired of trying, tired of adulting, tired of pretending, tired of preparing meals, tired of merely existing and going through the motions. We are plain *tired*.

You do not have to neglect yourself to be a good person. It's not always possible to get away, so sometimes we have to be creative about finding ways to take care of ourselves.

For example, at some point in the very near future my kids and I are going outside. We have a huge yard, and it serves us well. The kids will be fully equipped with water guns, sidewalk chalk, a hula-hoop, a scooter, sticks, leaves, acorns, pine cones, popsicles, frozen grapes, crackers, water bottles, a kickball, gardening toys, and a trampoline. I will sit in my lawn chair with ice-cold sweet tea and a book. The tiny humans will be instructed not to talk to me unless some part of their body is broken or bleeding. *Et voilà*! Self-care and parenting *perfected*. Try it and thank me later.

Self-care doesn't have to cost you any money; just do something that allows you to unplug and unwind. Sometimes that looks like trying out a new cupcake recipe, or bingeing your favorite show, or repotting your indoor plants, or taking a walk in a local park with lots of cool trails. Other times, self-care looks like a lazy weekend at home with family. No Little League games. No overstimulating birthday parties. No schedule to follow. Sometimes that's all you need. How are you recharging your batteries, friend?

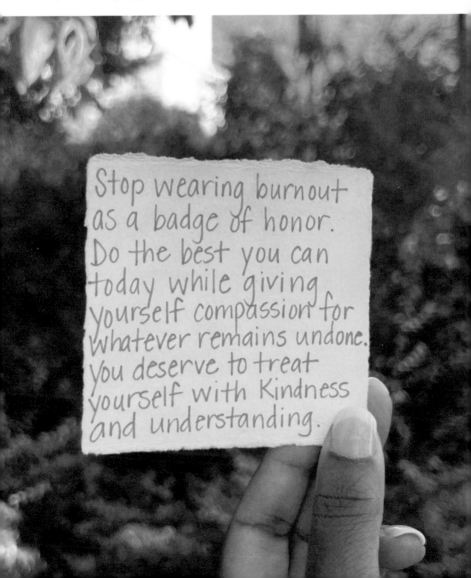

Stop wearing burnout as a badge of honor. Do the best you can today while giving yourself compassion for whatever remains undone. You deserve to treat yourself with kindness and understanding.

DAY 33

# Breathing Room

On Day 1 of my self-care plan toward living joyfully, I wrote:

*I deserve self-care. I deserve to do things that make me happy. I'm tired of neglecting myself and taking care of everyone else. I'm going to:*

- *Start a garden because I love plants.*
- *Take a Zumba class three days a week.*
- *Use my new mixer to bake my way through the cookbook that's been sitting on the shelf collecting dust for months.*
- *Join a book club and commit to reading two books a month.*
- *Volunteer at the women's shelter every week.*
- *Schedule weekly date nights with my husband.*

On Day 8 of my self-care plan, I scrawled this entry:

*What in the world was I thinking?*

Been there, done that?

I'd gotten sick and tired of being sick and tired. I'd gotten fed up with always being last on my to-do list. And when I started Day 1 of my self-care plan, in a defiant act of rebellion, I planned all the things I was gonna do to take back my power and reprioritize my life. But one week in, I was completely discombobulated, running around in a frenzy trying to fit in all the things that were supposed to make me happy but were actually driving me crazy.

What I wanted was quality time for myself—time to relax, time to play. What I got was a hundred more things added to my already overflowing plate. More stress. And confirmation that there just isn't enough time in the day for me to take care of *me*. Know the feeling?

So how about a different approach? How about removing unnecessary things from your plate that steal your time and energy? How about committing to only the most important things and leaving space for spontaneous adventures? How about allowing some of your time to be unscripted and unscheduled so that you have breathing room to make choices that nurture you? Because you deserve to be happy.

Self-care isn't always about adding more things to your life that will make you happy. Sometimes it looks like letting go of things, behaviors, and relationships that subtract value and joy from your life.

# You Need Rest

Full transparency: oftentimes my heart is heavy and my spirit is over-whelmed. And as much as I'd like to go out and "fix" it all, I know that I need rest—physically, mentally, and emotionally. I am more effective when I am rested than when I am weary.

Your worth as a human being is not determined by how over-whelmed, overbooked, and burnt-out you are. You have to be intentional about slowing down. You were not meant to live at warp speed, and the pace you've been trying to maintain isn't sustainable. It can lead to burnout, feelings of hopelessness, and giving up. So give yourself permission to pause. It is important to acknowledge that taking a break and giving up are not the same.

When things feel overwhelming, ask yourself what your mind, body, and soul need in that moment. What nourishes you and gives you life? What brings you joy and excites you? Spinning your wheels won't get you any closer to achieving your goals. Most days, I have plans to do *all the things*. But my body and my spirit often say, *"No, ma'am. Get somewhere and sit down."* Maybe you need to do the same.

Let's all agree to stop:

- Running ourselves into the ground
- Feeling guilty about giving our bodies, minds, and souls the rest they need
- Letting society tell us that being miserable and burnt-out makes us "good moms," "good wives," "good employees," and so on.

Taking up space in the world right now can be exhausting. So my advice if you're feeling weighed down is allow yourself to pause and *rest*.

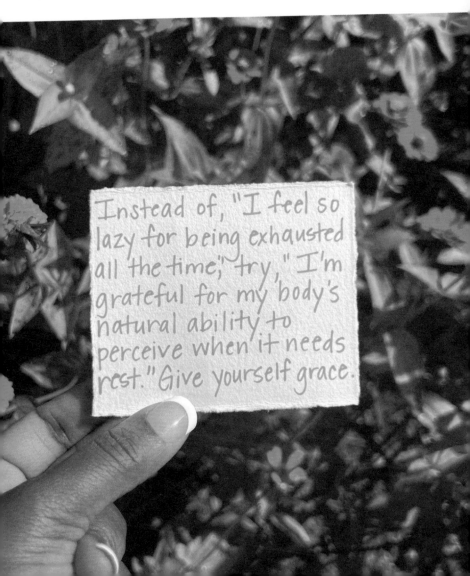

Instead of, "I feel so lazy for being exhausted all the time," try, "I'm grateful for my body's natural ability to perceive when it needs rest." Give yourself grace.

# Look After Yourself

I'm sure you've heard the phrase, "You are your own worst critic."

Even when people compliment me on a job well done, I immediately begin downplaying and minimizing whatever it is I've accomplished. Or I try to give the credit to someone else.

If I'm not intentional, my internal dialogue begins to take on the same dismissive tone:

- *I really don't have the qualifications for that position. I shouldn't waste my time submitting an application.*
- *It's been years since I worked in that industry. So much has changed. I wouldn't fit in there.*

What is your internal dialogue like? Think about what you think about. When you consider trying something new or different, what are the first thoughts that come to your mind? Are they encouraging? Life-giving? Uplifting? Or do your thoughts morph into a detailed spreadsheet, complete with graphs and charts listing all the reasons you'd be unsuccessful?

When I'm trying to frame my thoughts in a healthy way, I find it helpful to imagine myself having a chat with a good friend and thinking about what I would say to her. If my friend told me she was thinking about taking a leap of faith and pursuing that thing she's always wanted to do, I would share enthusiastically in her joy and excitement. I would show genuine interest and ask her questions about it. I would ask her what I could do to help her during this transition.

Be willing to take care of *you* just as much as you take care of everyone else.

You deserve to be cared for and looked after. It's not selfish, and you do not have to feel guilty. You were not meant to limp through life tired, undervalued, and frustrated. You wouldn't let your loved ones walk around thinking they were insignificant and unimportant. Don't do it to yourself either. You are important. It's okay to love *you*.

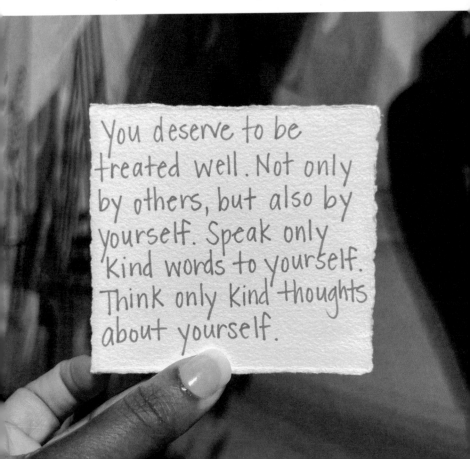

# A Rested Mind

It seems as though depletion and utter exhaustion have become the standard by which we measure accomplishment. Sometimes, it's almost as if I'm playing a little game with myself: *How far can I push myself before I completely lose my mind and lash out at everyone around me?*

You often have to get to an unhealthy place in order to know you should have stopped yourself a long time ago. But the problem with using burnout as an indicator of your limits is that once you're there, you've done some damage. You've lost your temper, hurt innocent people's feelings, and probably have a few apologies to make.

So where do we even begin to make our way back to ourselves? To get the rest we so desperately need? To begin to see ourselves as human beings worthy of love, consideration, and grace? Perhaps we start with *admitting*. Admitting the jig is up—that we're overworked, overwhelmed, and overcommitted. That we use our productivity as a measure of our overall worth. That we're addicted to performing not only for others but also for ourselves. That taking a step back and slowing down feels scary because it means we have to spend time with the messy parts of ourselves that we're afraid to confront.

And how do we move on to grace? To extending grace to ourselves and others? By allowing ourselves to be less than perfect. Allowing ourselves to rest because it's necessary for our overall wellness, rather than offering it to ourselves as a consolation prize only after we've suffered and neglected ourselves or lashed out at others enough. Give yourself grace to be human, to be tired, to make mistakes, to try again, and to accept that you're able to do your best and give your best when you are replenished and full.

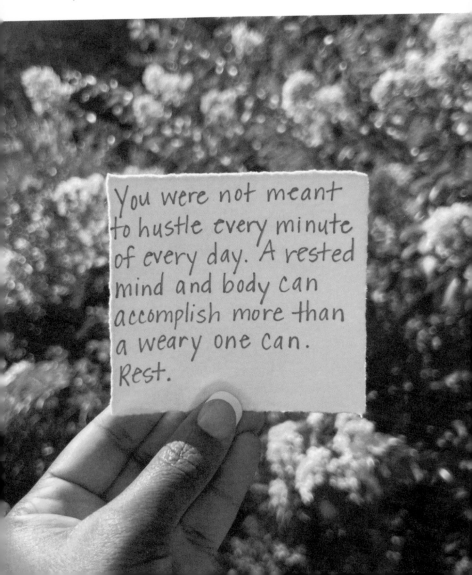

You were not meant
to hustle every minute
of every day. A rested
mind and body can
accomplish more than
a weary one can.
Rest.

# You Deserve Rest

Let's just be honest. Sometimes the truth is that no matter how self-aware we are, no matter how well-adjusted we are to the idea that self-care is essential and that setting realistic expectations for ourselves helps to combat burnout, anxiety, depression, and a host of other mood disorders, there is something inside us that will overschedule and overcommit ourselves until we fall apart. That something inside us desperately needs to prove our worth, our value, and our right to take up space in this world. It makes us believe that if we are constantly producing and being efficient and accomplishing and over-extending and showing up for everyone and picking up all the slack and filling in the gaps and being the one everyone can count on, then and *only* then are we worthy of the space we occupy in our homes, our jobs, and our communities. Only then are we worthy of some of our own time. Only then are we worthy of taking a break or a nap or even entertaining the idea of telling someone "no."

But you deserve more than scraps at the end of the day. You deserve to save some of you for you.

Will you feel guilty? Maybe. Will you feel like you let someone down? Perhaps. Does it feel good? Not always. But you need that quality time for yourself. As much as you take care of others, I encourage you to also advocate for and honor your own self-care. Sometimes self-care is saying a polite "no" to a good thing, because that good thing in a certain moment is not good for you. And that is okay.

In the same way that we prioritize feeding our physical bodies, we must be intentional about making the time to nourish our spirits as well. Take some time to get quiet, block out the noise, and listen to what you need holistically. You deserve rest.

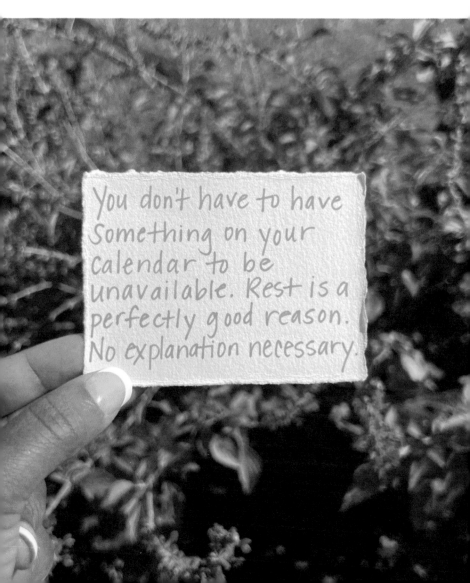

You don't have to have something on your calendar to be unavailable. Rest is a perfectly good reason. No explanation necessary.

# Superwoman's Day Off

Dear Superwoman,

A cape is a costume. It's okay to take it off sometimes. You can't play dress-up forever.

You are allowed to be human. To be tired. To ask for help. To make *you* a priority. You cannot pour from an empty vessel. Work on being mentally, spiritually, emotionally, and physically healthy so that you can give your best to yourself and to others. Invest in *you*.

Start by releasing the tension in your body that you don't realize is there because you're so used to it. Close your eyes. Pay attention to where those random aches and pains are. Notice your breath. Inhale. Exhale. Put your hand on your chest and feel your heartbeat. Breathe in. Breathe out. Feel the air entering and exiting your lungs. Focus on your breath, and relax your mind. Let all those anxious thoughts leave your mind as you exhale. Take as much time as you need.

*Resist* the temptation to be Superwoman today. Yes, you are capable. Yes, you are a strong woman. Yes, you can multitask like a *boss* and handle anything that life throws at you. But that doesn't mean you *should*. Allow yourself the space to gracefully decline anything that is unnecessary and disruptive to your overall well-being. Be intentional with your time and energy, because it is precious. Let some things *go*.

Let Superwoman have a day off. Trade your cape in for a weighted blanket, and take a nap.

What you've been
trying to carry is too
heavy for you. Put some
of it down. Take a break.
Relax your shoulders.
Unclench your jaw and
fists. Take a few long, deep
breaths. You're going to
be okay.

# Love from a Distance

If you've ever gone on a group vacay or family trip, you already know: you cannot travel with everybody. Not everyone has the same interests, goals, motives, or attitude that you do. Not everyone's spirit and intentions will align with yours. I'm not gonna call out anyone specific, but you know who you are.

Drama and confusion tend to follow certain people. When you're with them, you're bombarded with gossip, negative attitudes, and pessimism. It seems everything in their life is going wrong, it'll never get better, they're unhappy, no one cares about them, and everyone is out to hurt them. They don't want your help or suggestions and are determined to remain stuck in the misery of their own minds. It can make you feel helpless.

Have you been there? You planned to take a break from work and enjoy downtime with a friend. But you leave your get-together in a worse mood than the one you went in with. You feel depleted and have to go back to work to deal with the difficulties with a grumpy attitude. You do not feel better, and you regret spending that precious portion of your time being drawn into someone else's whirlwind of confusion.

Remember this: where there is clarity, there is peace. What you're holding on to might be holding you back. You can choose to honor and protect your mental and emotional well-being by lovingly distancing yourself from relationships that are draining, inconsistent, or possibly toxic. Not everyone we love is capable of maintaining a healthy rapport with us. Sometimes we gotta lace up those sneakers and walk (or run!)

away. It doesn't make you unkind, selfish, or disinterested. You can be a caring, sympathetic person and still maintain a healthy distance between yourself and negativity. You can love from a distance.

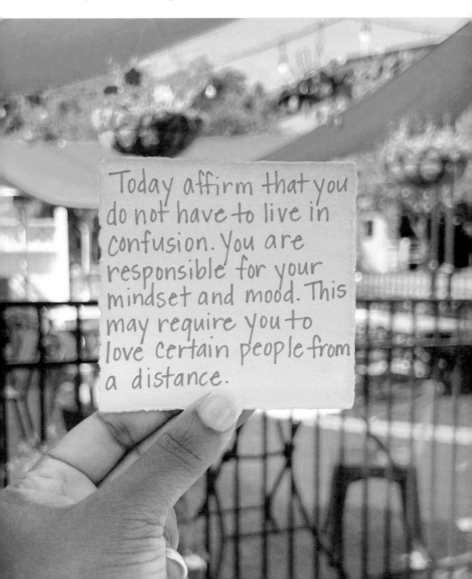

Today affirm that you do not have to live in confusion. You are responsible for your mindset and mood. This may require you to love certain people from a distance.

# Know Your Limits

How many things on your unending to-do list are put there by other people? How many times do you say "yes" or "maybe" when you know your plate is already full? How many times have you neglected your emotional and physical well-being to accommodate others, only to be left feeling empty and overwhelmed with regret? How many nights do you lay in bed feeling depleted and in tears because you did everything for everyone else, and now you have no energy or motivation to do anything for yourself? And how many times have you promised yourself you would say "no" next time, only to be guilted into saying "yes" yet again? I don't have enough fingers and toes for that count! But I'm learning to admit and accept my limitations. I have only so much time and bandwidth, and there is nothing wrong with honoring that line.

You can be friendly, empathetic, and considerate —*and* respectfully decline what doesn't align with your values, your spirit, or your schedule. Choosing to set and maintain healthy boundaries does not reflect poorly on your character. Quite the opposite. You simply recognize that because your time is limited, you must limit the amount of time you spend on extraneous things.

Setting boundaries shows you are self-aware. Saying "no" means you know your limits. Saying "no" to the unnecessary means you have the time and energy to say "yes" to the things that are really important to you. Saying "no" means you are taking back your free will. You are taking back your power and your right to choose how you invest your resources.

Start by taking small steps in the right direction: Don't lie. Don't make excuses. Don't overexplain yourself. Just politely decline. Those who really matter will understand, and you will be a happier, healthier, more balanced person as a result.

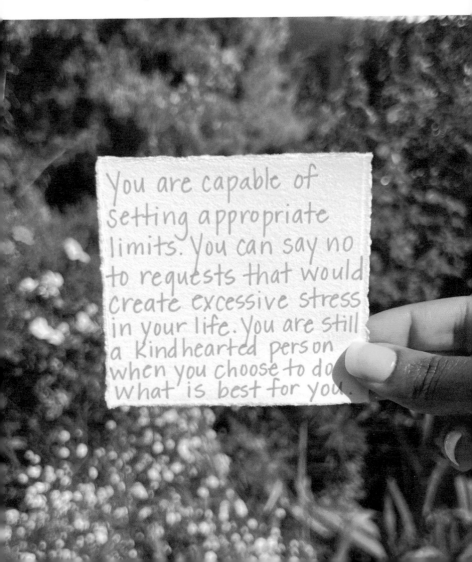

You are capable of setting appropriate limits. You can say no to requests that would create excessive stress in your life. You are still a kindhearted person when you choose to do what is best for you.

# Refuse Guilt

We know the drill, y'all. Here's how things usually go for many of us (feel free to insert any personal variations that are true for you):

1. You finally get fed up with your family's antics.
2. You declare loudly that you are taking long overdue time for yourself.
3. You spend too much time figuring out what you'd actually enjoy doing.
4. You prep everyone before you leave and answer a million questions.
5. You feel proud that you advocated for yourself and prioritized your needs.
6. You feel guilty and start thinking about all the things on your to-do list you could be getting done.
7. You realize that your precious alone time is already over, and you still feel empty.
8. You go back home to your people in a bad mood because you wasted a perfectly good opportunity to refill your cup.
9. Rinse and repeat.

Let's change that, friend. You deserve that time. Try this approach instead:

- *Immediately name any feelings of guilt that may come up about taking time for yourself.* Because they will come up. You've been taking care of everyone else and neglecting yourself for years. This is something new—it might feel weird. Write those thoughts down and move forward.

- *Resist the urge to always be busy.* Not every task needs to be completed today, even though your inner critic may have tried to convince you it does.
- *Accept that taking a break is productive.* Yes, you could be getting things done, but when you engage in interests you enjoy, you're more likely to have lower stress levels, a lower heart rate, and a better mood. When you take a break, you get more done well.
- *Embrace the idea that self-care provides the stamina you need to take care of others.* Self-care gives you the capacity to do what you do for your people without resentment.

Change the drill. Give yourself a break, and allow yourself to fully benefit from it. I am. Self-care refreshes you and the people you are caring for.

# Reframe Your Thinking

I remember when my thinking shifted. I was overcommitted, frustrated, and resentful. I was tired of working so hard to please everyone around me and being devoid of the motivation or energy to take care of myself. I'd had enough! Something had to change, and I knew that it was my responsibility to start seeing myself as a priority.

If you're in a similar situation, then it's time for a mindset shift. We often see taking care of ourselves as taking away from those we care about, but it doesn't have to. We are most effective when our cups are full, and it's best to give from our overflow rather than our deficit. When we give ourselves what we need, we are less likely to respond in anger, resentment, or irritation when someone asks something of us. People don't need us doing something for them begrudgingly or out of obligation.

It is essential to your mental health and wellness that what you choose for self-care actually benefits you. Make sure it works for you and is in alignment with what your mind and body needs. It doesn't have to be trendy, but it does need to make sense. If you don't like being touched, don't force yourself to get a massage or a mani-pedi. If large crowds cause you anxiety, it doesn't make sense to spend your money on concert tickets.

Maybe you've always wanted to take a class on floral arrangements. Maybe you have a favorite at-home spa kit with a body scrub and mousse that makes your skin feel like butter. Maybe you like to volunteer at the local soup kitchen or women's shelter. Maybe you've been putting off registering for that 5K. Maybe your happy place is in the kitchen, and you're just itching to take that new Bundt pan out for a spin. Whatever it is, the time you spend nurturing yourself is valuable. You get to define what *care* means to you.

Be prepared. Write down five self-care activities you'd like to try over the next few months. Then make time to do them!

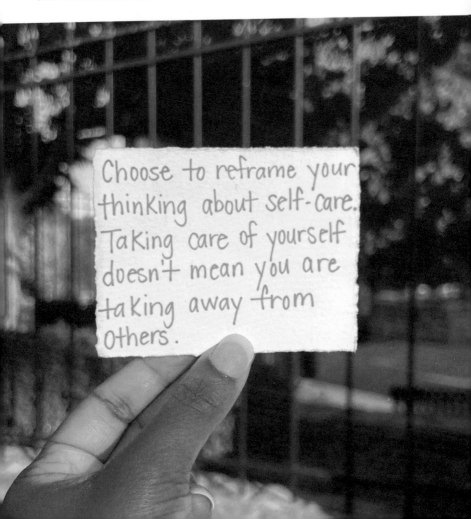

# Show Up

I can be a blessing to others while waiting on my own blessing.

Being able to shift my perspective is a powerful self-care strategy for me. Far too often, I get caught up in my wants and needs, trials and tribulations, failures and fears, and I forget to consider that the people around me are dealing with their own stuff. When I'm preoccupied with everything in my life, it's easy to feel hopeless and burnt-out. This is my signal to shift gears, to find something to focus on other than myself. To consider that doing something thoughtful for someone else and seeing them smile can infuse joy into my day.

We can't help others when our focus is solely on ourselves and our present circumstances. We never know how close someone is to giving up or giving in. Sometimes we just have to show up for each other, because most people don't know what they need when they're in the midst of falling apart. Look around. If you see a friend who is struggling, consider some of these suggestions:

- Send or drop off dinner.
- Send a handwritten card in the mail.
- Drive carpool for them or take the kids on a Saturday.
- Offer to sit and listen.
- Validate (and don't minimize) their feelings.
- Suggest they talk to a doctor or a mental health professional, and offer to go with them.

You can even volunteer to serve at a charity in your community. Local food banks and community gardens are great places to start.

Remember, you can be a light for someone even when things in your own life don't look very bright. Showing up for others is often part of your own self-care.

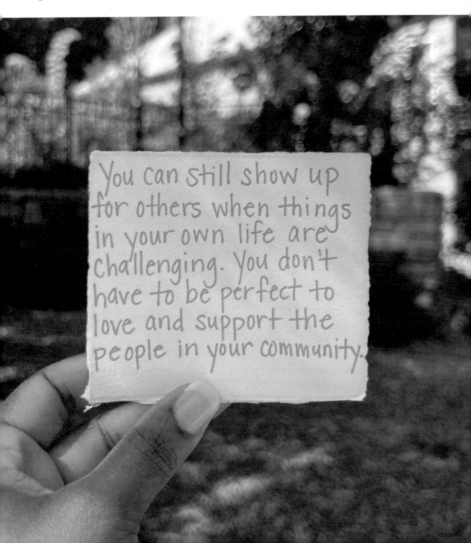

You can still show up for others when things in your own life are challenging. You don't have to be perfect to love and support the people in your community.

# Release Control

Raise your hand if you have control issues. I'm raising both of mine. I love schedules, lists, and rules. Planners, parameters, and procedures make me giddy. Why? Because it tells me there is order, there is a plan, and the plan will be followed. It gives me a sense of certainty and security. Ultimately, routines help me feel safe. I can predict at any given moment what is supposed to happen, and I won't be caught off guard by any tomfoolery. I love consistency. I do not love surprises.

Life has a way of showing us that we can choose to be flexible and bend, or be rigid and snap. When my husband and I both lost our jobs within a two-month period and didn't know how we'd pay for our daughter Bean's next gallon of lactose-free milk, much less the next mortgage payment, we quickly learned the concept of acceptance versus resistance. I had to choose to accept the shifts that were occurring in my life and be willing to pivot. No, the circumstances weren't fair. No, I hadn't done anything wrong. But refusing to accept the changes would have kept me stagnant and prevented me from growing into the person I am today.

When you resist change, no matter how uncomfortable it feels, you are also making the choice to resist growth. You make the choice that who you are and the life you have now is good enough. Playing it safe prevents you from attaining the possible bigger, brighter future. Don't rob yourself of the opportunity to discover something new. You are an exceptional person. Let go of control and discover your potential.

What you resist the most has the potential to change your life in a powerful way. Accept that you do not have to control everything, and you will still be okay.

# Practice Thankfulness

Sometimes we replay our problems over and over again so much that we accidentally make it a habit. Coffee dates with our girlfriends unintentionally morph into dialogues about how stressed we are; how the kids are tearing up the house; how our partners are less than perfect; how "if my boss makes one more sideways comment, they can *have this job*"; how "so-and-so is always smiling in my face, but she's so fake because I know that cryptic IG post she made was about me"; how there's never enough money to cover the bills; and the list goes on and on.

What if we were thankful for all the blessings and joy in our lives *despite* the problems we're facing? What if we were grateful for the problems—the messy kids, the imperfect spouse, the job, the option to unfollow a "friend"? When we practice gratitude, it opens our hearts to believe we will always have what we need, exactly when we need it.

That's when you must choose to shift your focus to the gifts that are so generously scattered throughout the moments of your life. Like how Bean peeks into my office after school to check on me and massages my shoulders when I look stressed. How she's the perfect big sister and helps so much with her brother. How she used her own money to buy me a slice of red velvet cake from the bake sale because she knows it's my favorite.

What you focus on is what you see. The thoughts you recirculate through your mind are the ones that dictate your mood. If you are ungrateful, you will constantly have something to complain about. Appreciate what you have, and you will attract more positive things into your life. Practice thankfulness.

Approach today with a mindset of gratitude. Be grateful for what you have, who you are, what you're learning, and where this journey is taking you.

# Prioritize Your Time

So sometimes—wait, who am I kidding?—*a lot* of times I am super ambitious and put a ridiculous number of tasks on my to-do list for the day. I stare at that beautifully curated list, energetic and lively, all colorful and accessorized with stickers, and immediately feel defeated. *How in the world am I supposed to get all this stuff done?* I think. *Where do I even start?* Then I just sit there, hoping for inspiration to tell me what to tackle first. Which usually results in an embarrassing amount of wasted time and doing mindless tasks like placing an unnecessary online grocery order or deleting old emails in an attempt to cling to the facade that I've done something productive.

I get so caught up in not being able to do everything that I don't even consider the option of choosing a few of the most important or time-sensitive tasks and doing my best to complete those. I am an intelligent, educated, and successful colleague, wife, and mother of two who accomplishes the impossible every single day. I make tough decisions. Of course I can set priorities and focus on them.

I can already hear y'all: "Well, what if *everything* seems like a priority?" I get it. I ask myself the same question. And full transparency, my "priority list" usually goes through three or four revisions before I get to the final draft.

Sometimes life just happens. Time gets away from us, and we need to take the initiative to ask for an extension or an amendment to the deadline. *Gasp!* It's not the end of the world. It happens. No one's gonna put you in time-out. You're human. And you'll never know if you don't ask. But asking and possibly getting that extension is much better than giving yourself an ulcer trying to do it all. Do what you need to prioritize what matters most.

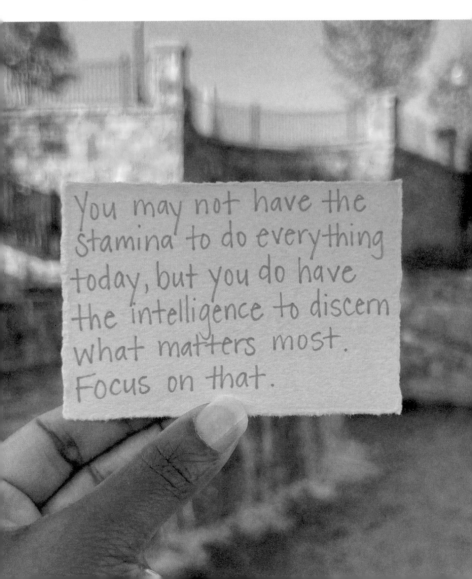

You may not have the stamina to do everything today, but you do have the intelligence to discern what matters most. Focus on that.

# Embrace Contentment

Let's clear up a common misconception about contentment, okay? Many times, people make the mistake of equating being content with settling. They are not the same.

According to the *Cambridge English Dictionary*, to *settle for something* is "to accept or agree to something, or to decide to have something, although it is not exactly what you want or it is not the best." And to be *content* is to have "a happy and satisfied feeling."

While you are developing into the person you want to become, you can choose to avoid being miserable about where you currently are in life. You can be optimistic and hopeful in the present while you work toward your future goals.

But it takes effort. Being a content person requires intentionality. That person cannot function on autopilot, or schedule every day down to the half hour, or behave as if her way is the only way to do something. That person doesn't rearrange cookie dough on the cookie sheet to make sure it's "right." That person might have pizza picnics in the middle of the living room floor. That person gives grace and doesn't expect perfection from herself or the people she loves. That person doesn't cringe at the way her husband loads the dishwasher, but rather she is immensely grateful for a spouse who is considerate and shares the load. That person accepts that knocking out her to-do list isn't always what she needs. Allowing herself to release control and enjoy some spontaneous moments of fun can help her grow into the woman who is receptive to joy flowing freely into her life.

# A Control Problem

Some days, I just don't wanna do stuff or think about having to do stuff. I'm trying to keep a mental inventory of how many rolls of toilet paper we have left. And the people in my house have the nerve to want to eat dinner every night! I don't want to have to be involved in all the decisions that need to be made. I want someone else to willingly take responsibility for some of these tasks so I can breathe.

So, my sweet husband says he will handle dinner, clean the kitchen, and put our son, Dominic, down for bed.

Not five seconds after I've run my bath filled with essential oils and lavender Epsom salt, put on my moisturizing face mask, and sunk down into the comforting warmth of the tub, my mind is bombarded with all the questions: *Will he make sure to include at least one vegetable with dinner? Will he remember to clean the kitchen counters with the disinfectant spray? Did he add water to the humidifier in Dom's room, sing him two songs, read* Goodnight Moon, *and turn on his sound machine?* Then a light bulb comes on! I realize that I don't have a "lack of help" problem. I have a control problem. I've created an entire narrative in my head about how I want things done. My husband is wonderful and loves to help, but he may not do things the way I would do them. He's showing up for me, and if he doesn't make a salad to go with the pizza he had delivered, the world is not going to explode. It's a "me" issue. If I want more downtime, I have to let people show up for me without interfering.

Do you have a control problem too? Do you sabotage your downtime by wanting all the control? Let's try to let go.

People won't always do things the way you do them, and that is okay. You can release the desire to control how others show up for you.

# The Self-Care Tool Kit

I've spent a significant amount of time over the years building my self-care tool kit. It's what I like to think of as my personal collection of coping skills that are available for me to use whenever life gets hectic or I need some additional attention and care.

Begin with a personal assessment of your emotional or mental state: How am I feeling right now? How do I want to feel? Then move on from feelings to actions: What can I do in the present moment to achieve the feeling or mood that I desire?

Depending on the emotions you named, ask these questions:

- Anxious/distressed/nervous: What makes me feel composed/tranquil/assured?
- Tired/droopy/exasperated: What makes me feel energized/invigorated/refreshed?
- Angry/heated/enraged: What makes me feel calm/peaceful/at ease?
- Sad/melancholy/sorrowful: What makes me feel joyful/happy/cheerful?

Once you have identified the emotion you're struggling with, it's time for a free-association brain dump! On individual slips of paper, spend a few minutes writing down every place, person, or activity you can think of that has helped you regulate difficult emotions in the past. Here are a few ideas:

- Names of restaurants, coffee shops, bakeries, and ice cream shops you love or want to try
- Shows or movies you love or want to watch
- A list of nearby parks with nice trails and beautiful scenery
- Aromatherapy candle scents
- Titles of books to read for fun
- Word searches, crossword puzzles, or sudoku
- Favorite snacks
- Sensory putty or fidget toys
- Journaling
- Mood-music playlist(s)
- YouTube playlist of fun dance, workout, yoga, deep-breathing, or relaxation videos

Gather them up. Dump them all into a supercute storage bin. Then when a particular emotion shows up, reach into the bin and pull out a slip of paper. Take time to engage in your suggested activity and allow yourself to de-stress before moving on to your next to-do list item. Thank me later.

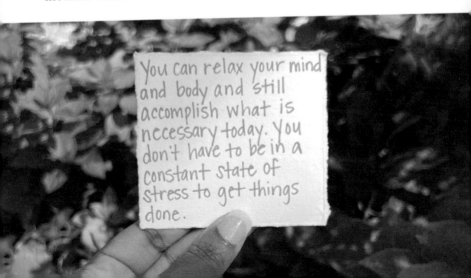

You can relax your mind and body and still accomplish what is necessary today. You don't have to be in a constant state of stress to get things done.

# Stop the Worry

Worry doesn't have to be our state of being. It may be a part of our experience, but it doesn't have to be the lens through which we view our lives. For many of us, worry is our default. I know it has been mine at several points in my life. It seems as soon as I get through a challenging situation like working from home with a sick toddler clinging to me, here comes something else I have to deal with. And if the situation happens to catch me off guard, I tend to use this silly logic: *If only I had anticipated the bad thing was going happen, I could have readied myself for it and not been so shocked and unprepared.* My bright idea is to "pre-worry." This logic asserts that if I pre-worry about things and contemplate all the possible ways that things can fall apart, then I'll be armed and ready when they do.

The problem with that line of thinking is that pre-worrying never, ever decreases the level of worry when the thing actually happens. It simply prolongs the total amount of time I spend worrying, because I didn't just begin to worry when that thing happened out of the blue. I worried in advance *and* when something actually happened. So I get to be a basket case for even longer than normal.

Maybe you have a similar story. Maybe your mind feels like an internet browser with a million tabs open at any given time. Maybe you're trying to plan so far ahead that you're using today's brainpower to worry about what could go wrong five days from now. The worrying isn't making you better. It's making you bitter.

You deserve to let your guard down. Your body and mind were not meant to withstand that debilitating level of apprehension. Take a breath. Give yourself permission to relax. It will be okay.

# Slow Down

Some days I feel completely overwhelmed. I'm overwhelmed by my job, by trying to be an engaged mother, by trying to be a present wife. On any given day I've started and abandoned eight different projects without crossing anything off my to-do list.

At the end of those days, I look up and realize I didn't eat any meals. I didn't drink any water. I probably had two cups of regular coffee, an afternoon iced coffee, a handful of Goldfish crackers, and a fun-size pack of Peanut M&Ms I found at the bottom of my work bag.

By the time the day draws to a close, my jaw aches from clenching it, my stomach growls angrily, and my neck and shoulders make popping noises anytime I attempt to move.

Have you ever been so consumed with what you need to accomplish—the big picture, the entirety of the project, the maze of logistics you have to navigate just to get through the day—that you lost sight of the day? Of the present? You have to get through today before you can even start on that deadline two months from now. Today first.

Remember:

You need to eat today.
You need to drink water today.
You need to take your meds and vitamins today.
Your family needs you today.
Your clients or coworkers need you today.

And also:
You deserve to love and be loved today.
You deserve to enjoy your life today.
You deserve to smile today.
You deserve to take care of your body today.
You deserve to prioritize your mental health today.
You deserve to rest today.

All the time you spend contemplating the future pulls you away from fully experiencing life in the moment. Slow down and take care of yourself.

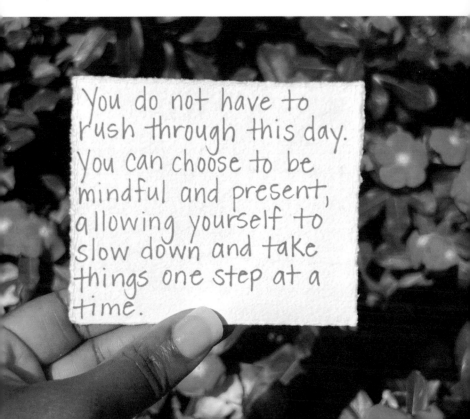

# Give Yourself Grace

After a hectic few weeks, I have every intention of resting and recuperating. I sit on the couch in my pajamas, fighting every little voice inside me that's telling me to get up and "do something." *Nope.* Not today.

We often won't allow ourselves to feel and acknowledge when we're getting close to our limit. And if we do happen to feel it—that inner knowing telling us to "get somewhere and sit down," as my Granny used to say—then we dismiss it, ignore it, or condemn it as a sign of laziness. We silence our inner voice, and we add just one more appointment to our calendar. One more email to send. One more phone call to make. One more social event to attend. One more favor to do. One more project to finish up.

Tomorrow I'll get up and do things, but today I'm allowing myself the grace to rest. To not feel bad about self-care and self-preservation. To not feel guilty about having my husband bring home dinner because I don't feel like turning the stove on today. And that's okay. Tomorrow I will be rested, and Bean and Dom will appreciate my renewed energy to deal with their shenanigans for the rest of the week. It's okay to take a break. It's okay to love yourself enough to rest. When overworking is the norm, your health and wellness suffer. What we really need—physically, mentally, and emotionally—is grace and compassion. We need to love ourselves with the same intensity that we love others.

Today commit to
giving yourself the
same grace you give
freely to others. You,
too, are worthy of
your own compassion
and friendship.

DAY 53

# Embrace Aloneness

Prioritizing self-care and creating space for what you need is easier said than done. And speaking from personal experience, it won't be as simple as flipping a switch. Retraining your brain is going to take time, but it can be done if you commit to the process.

First, name any feelings that come up about taking time for yourself. Because they *will* come up. Give yourself permission to feel those feelings and move forward.

Start small and work your way up. Schedule at least ten minutes each day just for you. Put it in your planner with fun stickers, or on your calendar with cute emojis. Get excited about it! Look forward to it! And protect that time slot like your life depends on it, because it does. Your joyful, fulfilling, gratifying life depends on it.

Timing is *everything*! Pick a time when you're least likely to be interrupted—early morning, lunch break, nap time, after your kids go to bed or while they're watching other kids play with toys on YouTube (#eyeroll).

What types of things might you enjoy during your alone time? Think of activities that help you relax, make you happy, make you laugh, energize you, or motivate you. You might consider pursuing a hobby, brainstorming discussion topics for the new small group you've been wanting to start, or spending some time out in nature. For me, it's diving into that new book series I've heard so much about.

Most importantly, please be gracious with yourself. Just because you finally decide to make time for yourself doesn't mean it will be easy or comfortable at first. Resist the temptation to focus on all the things you need to do. Reorganizing the pantry can wait. That thing you were supposed to do but you can't even remember can wait. Responding to that text can wait. But *you*, my dear, cannot wait. You've been waiting long enough. Your time is now.

Become comfortable with spending time alone. Value the opportunity and space to learn more about yourself and invest in your well-being.

# Play Is Okay

It's okay to smile. It's okay to be happy. Life doesn't have to be miserable and hard to be productive and meaningful. Treating yourself and having fun isn't silly or wasteful or irresponsible.

But as soon as I start believing all that, the questions begin to come: *What do I even like to do? What do I enjoy? What sounds fun? What is attainable in my current season of life? When did I stop playing, having fun, or enjoying life? And why?*

I'm pretty sure I have a history of dodging happiness. If I look as far back as my childhood, I remember priding myself on being a "good kid." The rule follower. The responsible one. The straight-A student. Dependable.

*Pleasure, happiness, joy, fun,* and *excitement* are not bad words. They are not selfish words. They are not frivolous or indulgent. They are a part of the abundant life I am meant to live. But in allowing other people's interpretations of the "right way to live" to become my guidebook, I neglected myself and forfeited the right to enjoy my life. Feeling stifled and repressed caused cognitive dissonance for me. Denying myself basic pleasures and happiness caused me to regret, to resent what I missed out on or didn't allow myself to participate in. And now, years later, I'm finally on a journey to figure out what I like and what makes me happy.

Don't be so concerned about being obedient and not messing up your life that you don't invest time into exploring what delights, thrills, or gratifies you. Taking time for play and hobbies is not a waste of time. Those things actually matter. They build up your soul so that you can face the harder side of life. It's okay to play.

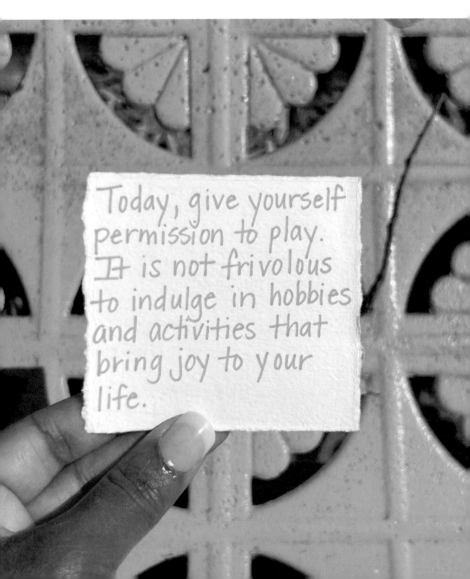

Today, give yourself permission to play. It is not frivolous to indulge in hobbies and activities that bring joy to your life.

# Temporary Interruptions

Some seasons of my life have been extremely hectic. So many beautiful yet unexpected opportunities have come my way. Because two things can be true at once, sometimes I feel both incredibly blessed and incredibly overwhelmed. Managing it all can be a tightrope walk. I suffer from bouts of chronic insomnia, and most days I wake up exhausted. One particular morning, I woke up feeling especially wretched, but in true overachiever fashion, I had every intention of pushing through and ignoring every bit of my intuition that was telling me to pause and take a break—because mental health professionals like me struggle with taking their own advice too.

As I sat at my desk, my eyes welling with tears while I stared blankly at my computer screen, trying to figure out which task to tackle first, my husband walked in and asked me what was wrong. I burst into sobs. Upon seeing my distress, he immediately wrapped me up in a hug as I cried into his chest. Once I had calmed down and was able to breathe, he sorted through my to-do list, gave me three tasks to complete, and told me to cancel anything else I had going on that day. Bean came in, saw me weeping, and wrapped me in the biggest hug her little arms could give. With all the love and empathy in her heart, she spoke some beautiful words of wisdom to me. Those words are the inspiration for today's note. May we all learn to let go, to regroup, and to give ourselves the grace to try again tomorrow.

This season is temporary, so it may be necessary to temporarily put some things down in order to make space for the priorities. You can always pick them back up when your capacity adjusts. Beautiful and unexpected things may be just around the corner if you will give yourself space to see them.

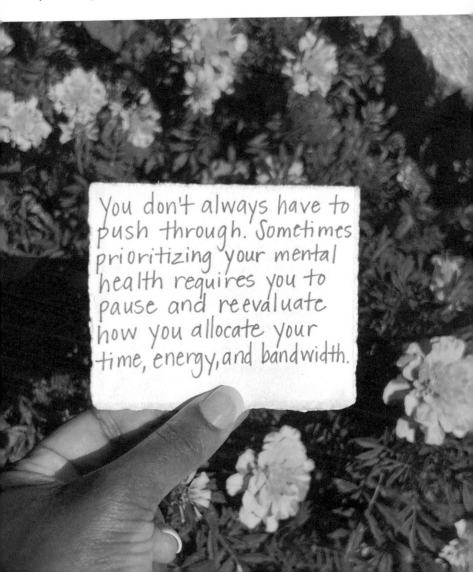

You don't always have to push through. Sometimes prioritizing your mental health requires you to pause and reevaluate how you allocate your time, energy, and bandwidth.

# Intentionality

If I'm not careful, my to-do list will get longer and longer every day and I won't even realize it. It's like I forget that every day of the week has the same twenty-four hours. I'm not going to magically get a few extra hours tomorrow to fold and put away laundry, reschedule that dentist appointment, or have a mommy-daughter date with Bean. But sometimes I can get so ambitious. I want to support my friends. I want to spend quality time with my family. I want my house to be tidy. I want the fridge and pantry to be full of wholesome ingredients to make nourishing meals. I want to snuggle under my weighted blanket and read for fun. I want to wash my neglected makeup brushes. In short, I want to do all the things, and there never seems to be quite enough time to accomplish them all.

Life is unpredictable and always changing. As soon as you think you have things under control, something seems to fall apart or needs your attention. You're being pulled in so many different directions that you don't know where to start because everything feels urgent. The deadlines are looming, and your mind is so frazzled, you want to avoid everything and take a nap. I get it; some things are nonnegotiables. But everything I say "yes" to means there will be less of me available for something else. So I have to be absolutely sure that my yeses are intentional and significant enough to justify the less of me that's left. There is only so much of me to go around. I have to take care of the essential people and responsibilities and not forget to reserve some of that precious time for myself—for replenishing what I am blessed to give every single day.

Do you let your to-do list get the best of you? Who are you saying "no" to in order to say "yes" to others? Who and what are essential? Prioritize your time to align with your essentials. And don't forget that time for yourself is one of the essentials!

# Replenishment

I don't like to admit it, but I am often skeptical of ease. It's almost as if I expect everything to be difficult or challenging. If it isn't, it's too good to be true. I feel nervous and uneasy when I designate time for a break or rest—I must be forgetting to do something extremely important, or I'm missing a deadline, or this is a trick and I really can't afford to be taking time off. Or if I take this time now, I'm gonna regret it when I'm frantically trying to get something done later. I'm gonna wish I had used this time "wisely" instead of wasting it.

Do you identify with this reasoning? Why is that, friend?

Why are we suspicious of ease? Why are we distrustful of simplicity? Where did we get the idea that everything has to be hard—that if it doesn't require struggle or a fight, something is wrong?

Aren't we worthy of rest? Don't we deserve tranquility in our lives? Spaces of serenity and calm are where we find peace and respite from the chaos of the world. These safe spaces are where we find margin to retreat and pay attention to the beating of our hearts. Where we take deep breaths, inhaling gentleness and exhaling restlessness. Where we slow down long enough to realize that what we've been losing sleep over really isn't as catastrophic as we're making it out to be. It's in those moments of slowness that panic subsides and allows us to see clearly what really matters, what is actually deserving of our time and attention.

So try it:

Inhale gentleness.
Exhale restlessness.
Inhale.
Exhale.

You're getting the hang of this replenishment thing!

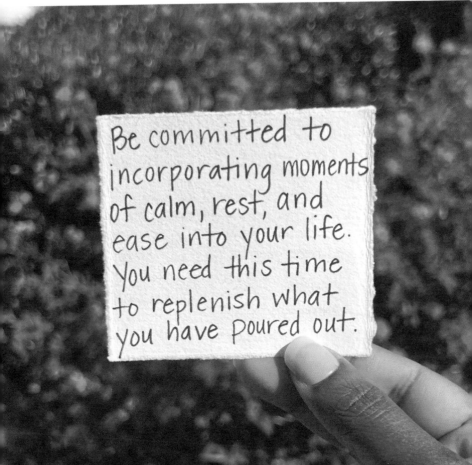

Be committed to incorporating moments of calm, rest, and ease into your life. You need this time to replenish what you have poured out.

# Trust Your Gut

As soon as a celebrity or famous person does or says something the masses dislike, an angry internet mob is campaigning to rip them to shreds and destroy their career—cancel culture is rampant.

Unfortunately, many of us apply the same mindset to our personal relationships. If someone backs out on a lunch date at the last minute or can't make it to your birthday party, they must not value your friendship. Or if that special someone promised to take you out for a date night, but their boss needed them to work late, they clearly don't see you as a priority, right?

Everyone makes mistakes. Mistakes are temporary missteps for which the offender shows remorse and penance. No one deserves to be canceled for one mistake. On the other hand, *behaviors* are patterns of actions that continue to repeat themselves despite the offender's awareness of the harm they cause. Recognize the difference.

Forgiving an oversight and giving grace is a natural, normal part of human interaction. But when someone's harmful behavior is repeatedly detrimental to you, and there is no attempt to stop that behavior or rectify the situation, your relationship with that person becomes unhealthy. Sometimes self-care looks like accepting that some of the people you love do not have the capability to love you back. You can do the inner work and come to a place of peace about the situation. You may even find empathy in your heart. But just because you've given them grace doesn't mean you have to allow them back into your space.

Listen to your instinct. When we become deaf to what our intuition is telling us, we often over- or underreact. Take the time to evaluate the behaviors of those around you, and use wisdom when deciding which people you allow to access you.

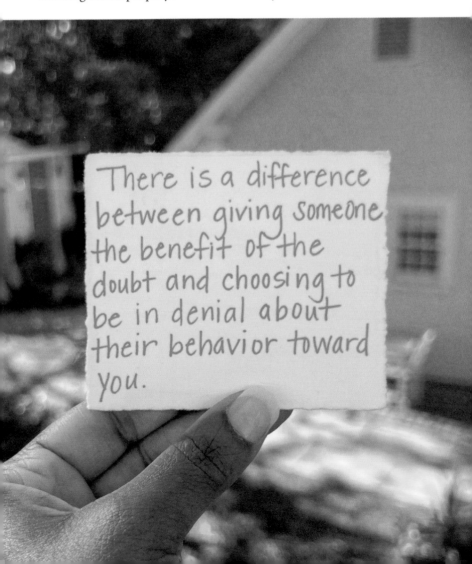

There is a difference between giving someone the benefit of the doubt and choosing to be in denial about their behavior toward you.

# It's Not Your Decision

I'm learning a very powerful lesson at this stage in my life: pause before I proceed. Instead of throwing myself into a situation, I'm seeing the benefits of stopping, breathing, and asking myself:

*Is that person or situation deserving of my time and attention? Has that person even asked for my assistance? Does that situation have anything at all to do with me? Do I have the capacity to add that situation to my plate right now?*

More often than not, the answer to all of the aforementioned questions is a resounding, "*Nope.*"

Would you have a similar response?

Could the pressure you feel be a direct result of inserting yourself into situations that have absolutely nothing to do with you? How much of yourself could you preserve and nurture if you stayed out of other folks' business and let them handle their own stuff? If you didn't attempt to be the hero when things get difficult for people and try to save them from normal discomfort or from the consequences of their own actions?

It can also be confusing when we consider how to move forward in our relationships. We struggle with finding a balance. How do we show up for our people without overstepping and depleting ourselves in the process?

I think we'd all enjoy a better quality of life if we released ourselves from the responsibility of repairing everyone's broken pieces.

So, repeat after me: "I can love and have concern for others without feeling the need to control or fix them."

You can relax and let others make their own choices. Your relationships will be better for it.

# Receive Goodness

I can count my friends on one hand. Oh sure, I know a ton of people. I meet a lot of lovely people in my line of work. But for me, acquaintances and friends are not the same. Friends get a level of access to me that acquaintances do not, because when I love, I love *hard*. It is a fiercely loyal, devoted, unwavering love. And as an introvert who is easily depleted by social interactions, I have to be intentional about where I invest my energy. I've come to accept that I simply do not have the capacity for small talk and surface-level chitchat. I'd much rather spend that time having meaningful conversations that are engaging and pour into me.

I accept that I am worthy of love and acceptance and dedication. I am worthy of those things not because I give them freely to others, but because I am a human being. It blesses my heart to see that the people I love and care about are happy, healthy, and experiencing beautiful and rewarding things in life. I always want the best for them. It's okay for me to desire and expect the best for myself as well.

You, too, are worthy. You deserve extraordinary things. You take care of so many people, investing energy, love, and time. Now it is your turn. Receive all the goodness that comes your way.

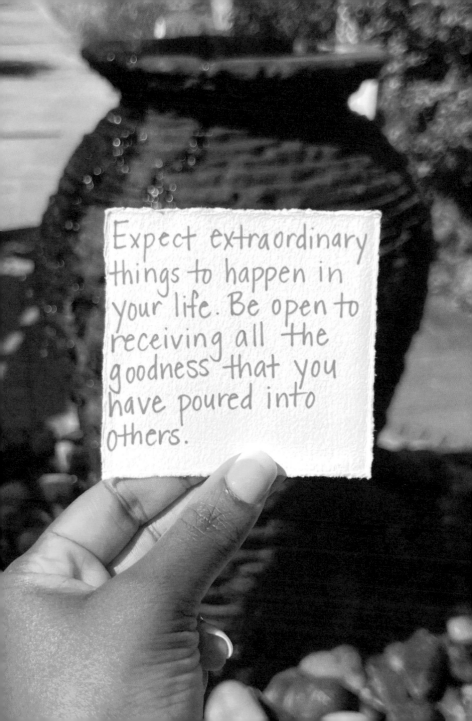

Expect extraordinary things to happen in your life. Be open to receiving all the goodness that you have poured into others.

# PART THREE

❖

# Shine
# Bright
# Anyway

❖

Your playing small does not serve the world. There
is nothing enlightened about shrinking so that
other people won't feel insecure around you. . . .
As we let our own light shine, we unconsciously
give other people permission to do the same.

—MARIANNE WILLIAMSON

# Fight for It

Last week the baby woke up with hand, foot, and mouth disease, there was a family funeral, our basement flooded, and I found water stains and mold on the kitchen wall. I thought I wasn't going to make it through the week. But I survived!

Maybe today was rough for you, but if you're reading this, it obviously didn't kill you. You're not going to prance leisurely through every day of your life. Some days you just have to celebrate the fact that you survived. And that's okay.

Is it worth fighting for? That friendship, that degree, that promotion, your health, your peace of mind, your family, your happiness? Are they worth it? If so, put on your big girl panties and fight for them. It won't be easy, but don't give up because you're not up for the fight!

Many of us are wrestling with hard challenges right now, and we'd love nothing more than to move right past them and onto greener pastures and better times. Part of what motivates us to remain strong and to keep pushing through it all is the hopeful anticipation of a better life with fewer hardships in the future. And that's understandable. We need that. We need to dream and hope that where we are is not where we'll always be and that the difficulties we face now are only temporary.

Every test, every trial, every challenge, every closed door, every "no," every heartbreak, every failure, every disappointment, every struggle, every sleepless night—*every single tear*—will not be wasted.

Be relentless in the pursuit of your dreams, because your tenacity and determination will get you through the hard times. Joy is coming.

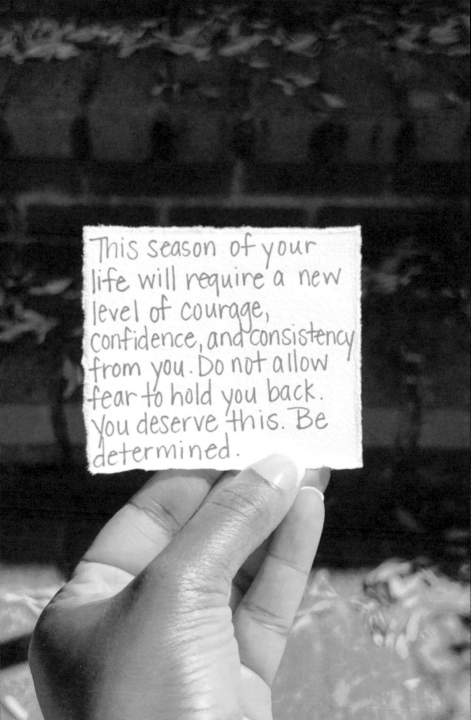

This season of your life will require a new level of courage, confidence, and consistency from you. Do not allow fear to hold you back. You deserve this. Be determined.

# Beat Fear

Just imagine how happy you could be if you spent more time enjoying life and less time worrying about the what-ifs or doubting yourself! Self-care starts in our minds. It begins with our thoughts and trickles down to every other aspect of our lives. If you're feeling discouraged and unsure about trying something different or pursuing a new opportunity, examine your thoughts. What types of things have you been thinking and believing about yourself lately?

These are some of the thoughts I fight against on a regular basis:

- *I could never do that.*
- *I'm not qualified to do that.*
- *I'm not educated enough to do that.*
- *I don't have the necessary experience to even try.*
- *I'm going to embarrass myself.*
- *I'm going to waste my time.*
- *I'm going to waste money and resources.*
- *I won't be successful, and then I'll regret making the decision.*
- *I don't deserve the opportunity—I've already used up all my chances.*
- *I already chose my life; I have to be a responsible adult and stick with what I've chosen.*
- *Other people may have the luxury of pursuing their dreams, but I have to be realistic.*

Does your self-talk sound similar? No wonder we feel paralyzed by fear! We don't always realize how many of our thoughts are dominated by negativity and apprehension. But don't worry; all hope is not lost. Changing your thoughts will change your life. Changing your inner dialogue from doubt and defeat to hopeful anticipation can transform who you are and what you believe is possible for you. It's time to be your own biggest cheerleader instead of your loudest critic.

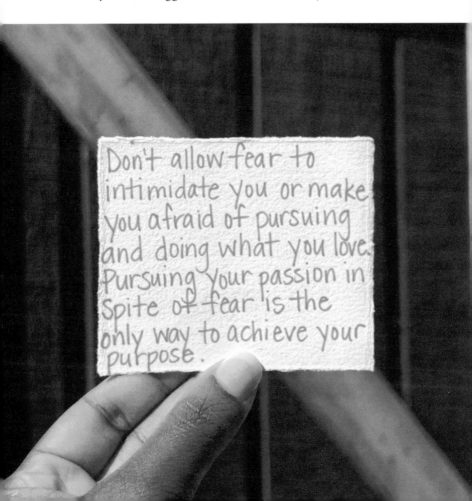

# Choose Joy

We want to feel that no matter how uncertain our circumstances might seem, we will be okay. That no matter what anyone else says or does, we have a choice in how things will end up. We want to trust that our lives and livelihoods and happiness and contentment and general state of being aren't left up to chance. We want to believe that we have a say in the whole matter.

In some cases we do. Unfortunately, in others we don't. There will always be things that happen in life that are outside of our control. Natural disasters. The choices and behaviors of others. The job market. The housing market. Traffic. The drive-thru line at Chick-fil-A.

I often tell Bean that the only thing in life we can control is ourselves: our behaviors, our attitudes, our choices, and our responses to what happens to us. But even more often, I remind myself of the same things. I can plan my entire life out to the second, but ultimately, the only thing I can control is myself and my response to the uncertain world around me. That realization takes a lot of pressure off me. It allows me space and grace to be human. It gives me permission to put down some of the unnecessary things I've been holding. It gives me a sense of peace.

You may not be able to choose what happens today, but you can choose to be joyful no matter what happens. You can choose to find the little nuggets of good. You can choose to be in control of your mood and mindset.

Let's do it together, friend. Start by writing down three things you can choose to be "joy-full" about today. Then repeat that one day at a time.

Today be joyful. You may experience pain, heartache, or frustration. You can still choose to keep your head up in spite of challenging circumstances.

# Your Words Have Power

Life is hard. And it is so, so good. Unfortunately, the hard parts of life don't ever feel good. And when we're in the thick of the hard, it's nearly impossible to see that any good will result. The hard parts are messy, "unfair," devastating, and even embarrassing at times.

Early on in my recovery, I realized I had to choose to define who I am, because if I didn't, the world would do it for me. Yes, I was in a devastating car accident. Yes, I live with ongoing symptoms of a concussion and traumatic brain injury. Yes, I experience chronic pain and other invisible challenges on a daily basis. Yes, these circumstances have changed the trajectory of my career and life in a major way. But that is only a part of my story. I won't let that part define the entirety of my life.

I could have allowed that situation to signal my defeat. To be the end of all my hopes and dreams. To destroy any semblance of a future for myself and my family.

But I wanted something different. I didn't know what that *different* was or what it looked like. And I certainly didn't know how to achieve it. I just knew that I could not stay where I was right after the accident. I could not be happy there. I didn't like how I felt there. And that had to change.

Changing how I spoke about my situation was the first step. Writing positive words about where I wanted to be rather than agonizing over where I was transformed my life. Those little notes of affirmation showed me my words have power, my voice projects that power, and I can choose to walk in the fullness of that power.

How will you use your words? Will you use them to predict your defeat or to declare your victory? The choice is yours.

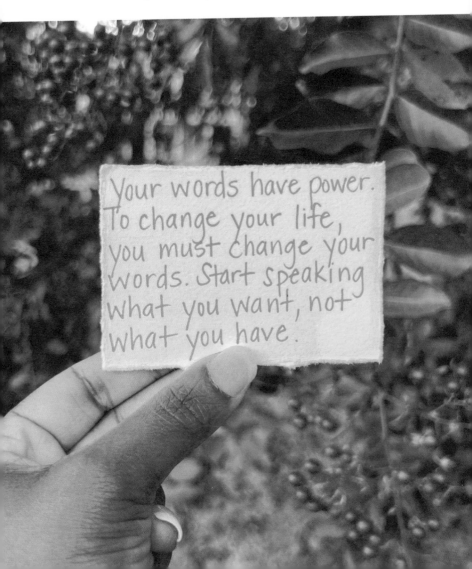

# Shine Bright Anyway

Communication is extremely important to me, so I've always been intentional about explaining and articulating my thoughts as clearly as possible. I've been teased and mocked for being "so proper" and I've even been accused of thinking I am "better" than others because of the way I carry myself. As human beings who experience a vast array of emotions, it can be easy for us to take things personally. To misinterpret someone's mood or behavior in our presence as some sort of reflection on us. *Maybe they don't like the way I speak. Maybe they think I'm not smart. Maybe they don't like the way I dress. Or maybe they just don't like me.*

But most often, other people's actions are not a personal attack on me. They are often a reflection of that person's life experiences, current circumstances, or past traumas. We may never know the extent of someone's challenges or the depths of the dark and messy spaces in their lives. We may never know the source of their loneliness, their anger, their bitterness, their resentment, or their jealousy. And quite honestly, we are not responsible for deciphering the intimate details of their lives.

We are, however, responsible for nurturing the light that is inside us, the light that makes us who we are and informs how we experience others and the world around us. It is our responsibility to cultivate that light and feed it with goodness, grace, compassion, and joy, to allow it to illuminate the sometimes sad and scary and uncertain world we live in.

As you go through your day, remember you are a light. And you may be the only light the seemingly unpleasant student, or coworker, or relative, or grocery store cashier sees that day. Maybe all they know is darkness, and your light causes them some discomfort. Let them deal with their stuff. Wish them well. Don't change who you are. Shine bright anyway.

# Focus on Priorities

When I worked as a school counselor, I realized quickly that in my line of work, plans could go out the window in a matter of seconds. In order for my day to go "as planned," 730 students (and sixty-plus staff members, for that matter) had to be emotionally and mentally okay. And in case there's any question, that *rarely* happened.

One afternoon, after an exceptionally challenging day of student meltdowns, I found out I was nominated for Professional of the Year by my peers. People left sweet comments about why they nominated me, many of which referenced things I was totally unaware of, such as, "I've never seen Mrs. Cade without a smile on her face. She gives so much love and attention to each student regardless of what her schedule is or what she has planned for the day. She is a wonderful and welcomed addition to our school."

I was dumbfounded! I had no idea my work positively affected others, because all I knew was how frazzled I always felt being pulled in a million different directions. It was a reminder to me to keep smiling, to keep being flexible, and to stop obsessing over my to-do list. I'm responsible for many things, but some are much more important than others. I have to be intentional and deliberate about setting my priorities.

At the beginning of each day, take time to identify your top priorities and brush off those unrealistic expectations you have of yourself. By focusing on being present and maintaining your boundaries, you can inspire others to shine brightly themselves.

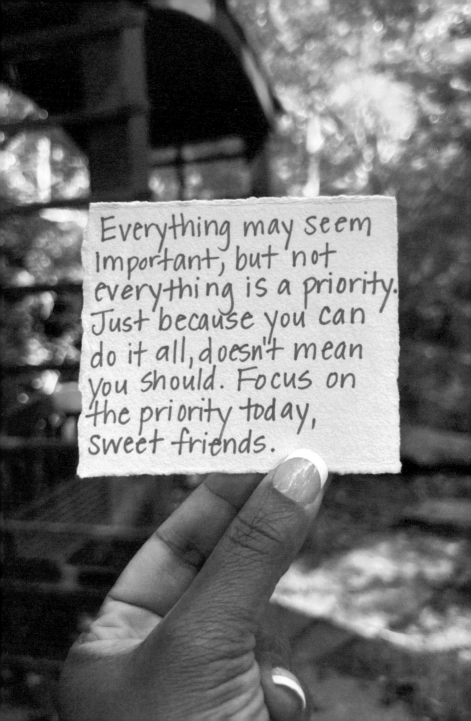

# The Possibility of Good

Inevitably, my day goes something like this: I get a call from the sweet front-office lady at Bean's school saying that while Bean was giving her friend a piggyback ride at recess, she tripped and fell face-first onto the cement. She has a large gash in her forehead, a chipped (permanent!) front tooth, and broken glasses. And just like that, welp! There goes my day. I can abandon all hope of getting my to-do list knocked out.

How many times do we say we're going to have a great day while simultaneously replaying all the ways yesterday didn't go as planned? Yeah, sure, we hope today will be better. But if someone asked us to put money on it, we'd bet that the day will have more of the same nonsense that derailed our plans yesterday. Actually, we'd be pretty surprised if today was a good day.

When I'm anticipating that yucky stuff will happen, nine times out of ten it does. When I start my day with positive expectations, however, I feel better. I am not saying my day is always perfect when I do this. I'm saying my mindset is open and I'm willing to be flexible even if things don't go according to plan. I notice the good things around me and find reasons to smile. I'm grateful for the person who held the door open for me as I rushed into school looking for Bean and the driver who let me merge into traffic. I'm able to find joy in the small things I might have otherwise overlooked or taken for granted.

So how are you going to think about your day? I challenge you to be intentional about finding at least three good things that made a positive impact on your mindset and mood. Look for the good possibilities. They're there if you're willing to notice them.

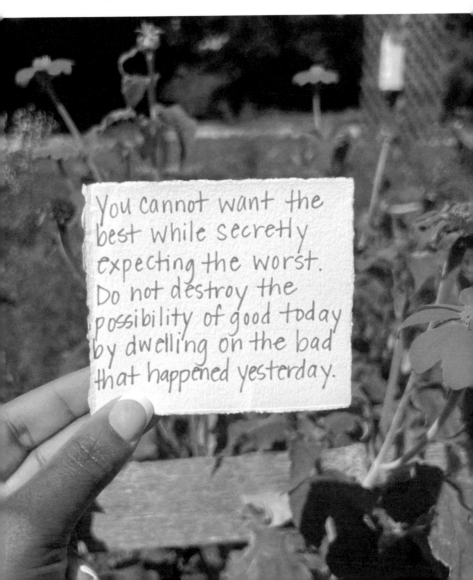

You cannot want the best while secretly expecting the worst. Do not destroy the possibility of good today by dwelling on the bad that happened yesterday.

# Believe in Yourself

Do you ever feel like maybe you shouldn't be doing what you're doing? Like maybe you've set your goals and aspirations too high? Like maybe somebody else—*anybody* else—could do it better than you? That even if you keep at it, you'll still fail? That if your past came to light, it would be all over?

Now let me ask you this: Does what you want and what you're willing to work for seem so incredible, so wonderful, so fulfilling and life-changing that you run away from it? Because you're sure something that magnificent could *never* happen to you? To justify your doubts, do you start making a mental list of all the reasons why you're unworthy or unqualified or unprepared to do what you feel called to do? Are you tallying up all your mistakes and weaknesses and keeping that number etched in your mind for safekeeping?

Friend, reminding yourself of your faults and how you can't do *(fill in the blank)* like you used to allows you to disqualify yourself before you even get started. It saves you the embarrassment of failing anyway. I never considered that I'd become an author. When the opportunity came for me to write this book, my mind rejected the idea before I could even say the word "no." I thought, *How am I in any way qualified to write a whole book?* And well, here we are. I've pushed past my fear and written a book. And I believe you can work through your fear as well.

Remember, as long as what you're hoping for, dreaming about, grinding for, losing sleep over, and pursuing is in alignment with the purpose for your life, then *you are meant to have it*. Stop doubting yourself.

You'll never get to the blessings if you keep running from the battles. Fight bravely through the challenges, and allow yourself to be transformed in the process.

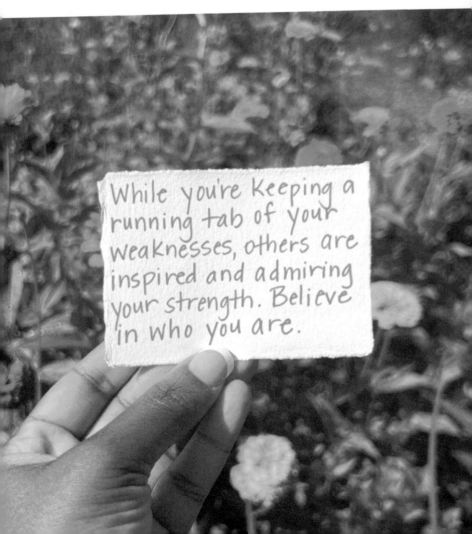

While you're keeping a running tab of your weaknesses, others are inspired and admiring your strength. Believe in who you are.

# Trust Yourself

Many times, living your truth means refusing to accept the narrative that is assumed about you. Maybe you've been labeled in the past as "too emotional" or "too sensitive." "Not strong." "Not gritty enough." For as long as I can remember, I've been labeled as "too nice" and told that I care too much about other people's feelings. And yet, I chose to channel my empathetic nature into helping others. It's what makes me an excellent counselor.

I'll be the first to admit that in a world that is constantly trying to make you into something you're not, it can be difficult to be true to *you*. Don't let drama, social media, keeping up with the Joneses, side-eyes, or disappointments stop you from being your best self and living out the purpose for your life. There is only one you, and the world desperately needs what you have to offer. Life is too short to wait for permission. The only thing standing between you and your dreams is that ridiculous excuse you've been telling yourself. Cultivate your gift and share it with those who need it most—it will reach the people it was intended to reach. Go out there and make the world a better place.

Your success may not get you five hundred thousand followers or fifteen thousand likes on every Instagram post. It may not yield a six-figure salary. It may not get you TV or podcast interviews with famous people.

But it doesn't have to. None of those things add to your worth. You have to be intrinsically motivated. If you're waiting on somebody else to validate you, value you, or approve of you to solidify your self-esteem, you'll be waiting for the rest of your life. Compliments from others can only make you feel good temporarily. Do *you* believe in *you*? Do you value *yourself*? Do you believe you are enough just because of who you are, not because of what you do or what you have to offer? Then TRUST yourself!

Stay Thoughtful.
Stay Resilient.
Stay Unbothered.
Stay Strong.
Stay True to you.

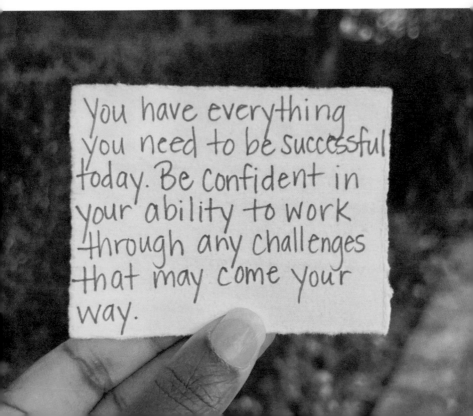

# You Are Incredible

Today I showered, put on real clothes, and applied concealer and a stunning, bold lipstick to be on Zoom calls all day. I got the kids up and off to school. I made sure I had all the ingredients to make dinner tonight. I took an actual lunch break instead of inhaling my food in front of my computer as usual. I finished up that work project and responded to those emails I've been avoiding. I didn't feel like it, but I did it.

Because we do so much, it's easy for us to overlook the tasks we accomplish every day. I've learned that in the midst of all the hard, unpredictable stuff, we must be careful not to miss the bits of goodness scattered throughout the day and the little glimpses of light that break up the darkness.

Start taking the time to acknowledge and celebrate just how exceptional you are. Stop and savor the moments when you feel good about yourself, rather than letting the messy parts of your present or past overshadow the beauty that's always been inside you.

Maybe you're the first in your family to graduate from college. Maybe you come from an environment where everyone expects you to fail, but you've beaten the odds and you are a phenomenal human being.

You are going to do something so important. Something significant. Something life-changing. Take time to admire your resilience and determination. Why? Because the stuff that's behind you is *behind you* for a reason. It doesn't determine where you're going *or* who you're becoming.

You are brave. You are strong. You are worthy. You are valuable. You are important. You are talented. You are incredible.

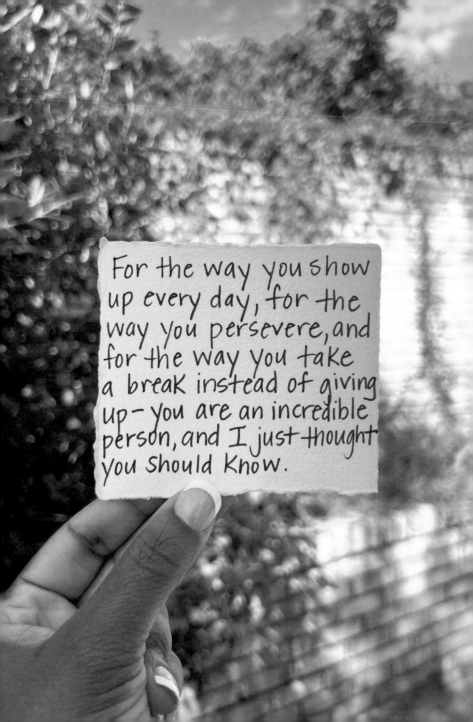

# Thankful and Tired

My child asked me to open a pack of fruit snacks and is now trying to squeeze that pack of fruit snacks to me through the crack below the bathroom door. He's annoying *and* adorable simultaneously. It's okay.

And it's okay if:

- You've reheated your fancy coffee for the fourth time this morning—because *life*.
- You're grateful for the paycheck that covers the necessities and even a few indulgences, but you resent that your boss expects you to respond to emails and phone calls after work hours and doesn't respect your personal time or boundaries.
- Your attempts at meal planning are epic failures because if you're lucky enough to remember to write a shopping list, trudge through the grocery store, and make it out alive with a fraction of your sanity, you're too exhausted to cook by the time you get home and end up ordering pizza for dinner. You will also be having leftover pizza for breakfast in the morning —with fruit, of course. Because #balance.
- You just need a few minutes a day when no one is talking to you, but you also want to be informed about all of the exciting things going on in your friends' lives.

Two things can be true at once. Learn to embrace the "and." You can love your children *and* need a break from them. You can be aware of all the things you need to do *and* know that you need a brain and body break. You can enjoy your friend's company *and* not feel up to that coffee date.

You don't have to pretend. Acknowledging your need for downtime doesn't nullify the gratitude you feel for your life and the people in it. Give yourself permission to live your full truth. The more you do it, the easier it'll become.

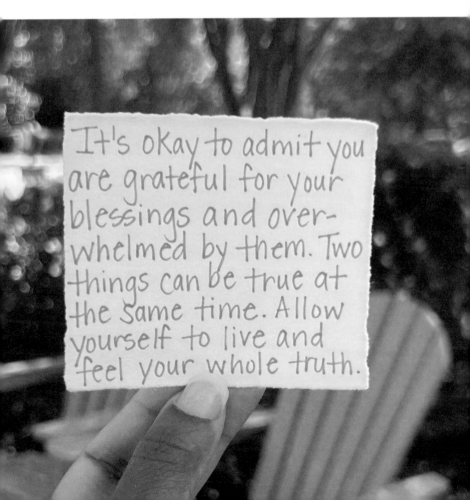

It's okay to admit you are grateful for your blessings and overwhelmed by them. Two things can be true at the same time. Allow yourself to live and feel your whole truth.

# Be Intentional

When Bean has tons of after-school activities, dinners need to be quick and easy, DIY-type meals. I do not have time to be soaking red beans and roasting whole chickens. Like my Granny used to say, "Ain't nobody puttin' a whole bunch of pots on the stove this week."

At some point, we've all wished we could get more than twenty-four hours in one day. And we've told ourselves that if we just had a few more hours in the day, we could get everything on our to-do lists done. That more time was the ultimate solution to our productivity problem. I'd venture to say that even if I had more time, I'd find more things to do and eventually end up in the same predicament.

We don't have an infinite amount of anything. As human beings, we have limits. Instead of being resentful, we can choose to work within the confines of our humanity.

Because I have only so much bandwidth, I choose to make conscious decisions about how that bandwidth is expended. I cannot afford to give attention to things that will drain me because there are spaces and situations in my life that require me to be fully present— and those things are important to me. It's about making choices. Doing a sort of cost-benefit analysis and then being satisfied with what I choose. When we have more free time in the evening, we can plan to have a picnic at the park or go to a restaurant for dinner or maybe roast that lemon and rosemary herbed chicken.

It's about being flexible and making adjustments when necessary. So pour yourself into the people and moments that matter most.

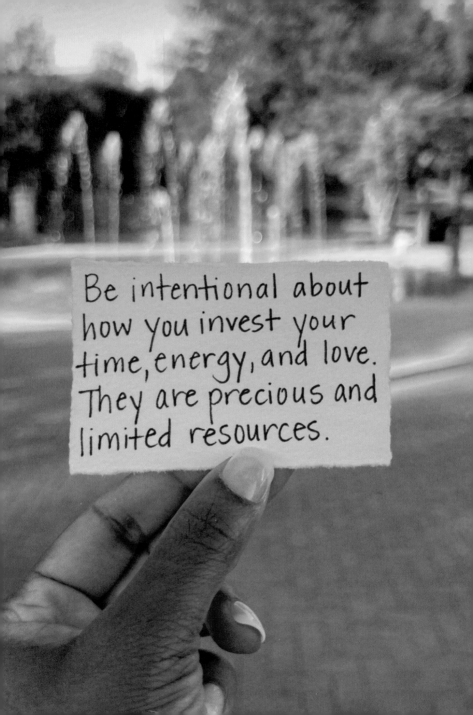

# Find Your Purpose

Every single day, we can make the conscious decision to get out of our own way. Every day, we can choose to trust in the power of our voices, the purity of our intentions, the kindness of our actions, the potential of our efforts, and the impact of our authenticity. We can choose to believe that we can take care of ourselves and serve others well. We can choose to believe that our words will reach the people who are meant to hear and receive them. We can choose to believe that we are enough, that we are making a difference, and that we are exceptional at what we do. We can choose to believe that our best is enough as we fulfill our purpose.

For those of you struggling to find your purpose, that "thing" you feel you were meant to do . . .

For those of you who know there's got to be more to life than what you're currently settling for . . .

Don't let all the reasons why something may not work keep you from starting in the first place.

When your heart and intentions are pure, you are equipped with what you need to utilize your gifts and talents. Stop doubting yourself and take that first step.

Sometimes we allow perfectionism to become a stumbling block between us and the pursuit of something great. No matter what you choose to pursue, it won't be perfect the first time. Just get it done and improve along the way. Someone is searching for exactly what you have. When you hold yourself back, you rob the world of the opportunity to experience your unique gift. If *you* don't believe you have something valuable to offer the world, no one else will.

Someone needs the light you have to offer. Please don't hide it just because it doesn't shine as brightly as you'd like it to right now. Your glowing flame is already bright enough to show someone a path through the darkness.

That thing that keeps you up at night. That idea. That dream. That's called purpose. And it's your gift to the world. Keep pursuing that. You can make your dreams your reality.

# Stronger than Ever

Even when I've had a rough day and I'm having a pity party on the couch in my comfy-but-not-cute pajamas at 5:30 p.m. and inhaling an entire tub of pimento cheese with a cold glass of sweet tea on the side, I can take a minute, regroup, and keep putting one foot in front of the other. I remind myself that I don't have to give up. That I can wake up tomorrow and try again. And so can you, sweet friend!

This test won't last forever. It can't. It is preparing you for something supernatural to happen in your life, something you hoped for but never dreamed could happen. Give yourself love. Give yourself time. Give yourself rest. Give yourself grace. But please, *please* don't ever give up. No matter what your inner critic says, you can get through this.

Even when things don't look good, they are working out for your good. You—yes, *you*! It's your turn. You can't possibly believe that everything you've been going through was all for nothing. You are going to walk out of this *stronger than ever*! So keep pushing. Your life is changing at this very moment. Have the courage and faith to believe it, even if you can't see it yet.

Whatever seems impossible in your life today, trust and believe that you can handle it. This isn't your first rodeo. As of today, you've made it through 100 percent of your bad days. You may be limping. You may have a hole in your favorite pair of black leggings. You may have some scratches. But you are still here, and that is enough.

# Comparison Blues

You've been so happy lately. You and your husband are growing together, communicating effectively, and life is good.

Until you get to the office on a random Tuesday, and your co-worker's husband has had ten dozen roses delivered to her desk.

That evening, your husband gets home from work, and you barely speak to him. He asks you what's wrong. You say nothing. Bless that poor man's heart! He's trying to figure out if there's a special occasion he may have forgotten about. But there isn't. There is only the resentment smoldering in your stomach, reminding you that your coworker's husband sent her flowers and yours didn't. You don't even like flowers! You're more of a cupcake girl.

Suddenly, your life feels insufficient. Your circumstances haven't changed; they just look different from someone else's. You've allowed comparison to invade your thoughts. Does this resonate with you? What do you observe about the lives of others that makes the gifts in your life seem a little less shiny?

I encourage you to resist the impulse to compare. It can be difficult when you're bombarded with carefully curated visual access to what others are experiencing. But you can get your mind out of that loop with a few simple adjustments:

- Be deliberate about the content you consume. Disengage with material that causes you unnecessary discontentment.

- Get serious about gratitude. Write down the people and things you're grateful for daily.
- Define what really matters to you, and be completely transparent with yourself. When you have clarity about what you want, your focus is on bringing those things to fruition in your life.

Become so excited to see your hopes and dreams materialize that you don't have the time to be concerned about other people's stuff. No one else's lifestyle will be able to cast a shadow on the beautiful life you have.

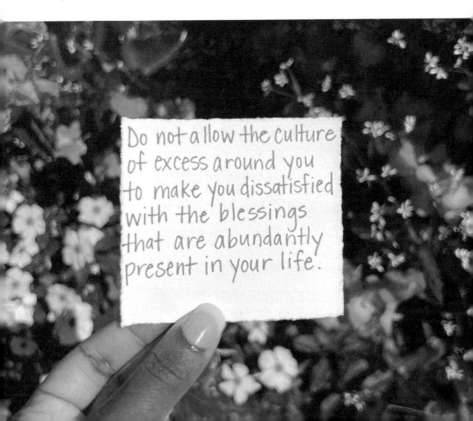

Do not allow the culture of excess around you to make you dissatisfied with the blessings that are abundantly present in your life.

# Push Through

For many years, I convinced myself that there was only one "right" way to start the day. My morning routine had to be the same every day in order to ensure success and optimal productivity. So when my schedule changed or my child got sick or there was an accident on the way to work, I became paralyzed with anxiety trying to maintain that routine, rather than choosing to be flexible and pivot. It was unhealthy, and I realized that I had to let go of that way of thinking.

Doing the same old thing keeps you in the same old place with the same old mediocre life. So, what if you make yourself uncomfortable, push through the fear, and embrace the awkwardness of an unfamiliar routine? What's on the other side could potentially change your life.

Life is constantly changing, and sometimes change feels uncomfortable. So we fight and resist the change that could be so good for us. We kick and scream. We try to run away from life's essential pruning process. But the truth is, we need to trim some of that dead weight. We need to let some things go. It may hurt like nobody's business, but it is so, so necessary.

Once you've done the work, made those tough decisions, and walked away from the situations that weighed you down, you will wake up one day and realize how good you feel. How relieved you are. How much easier you can breathe. How the anxiety and depression are no longer debilitating. How you have a greater capacity to love and be loved. It's amazing how that happens, isn't it? When you allow some temporary discomfort to drop-kick you out of your comfort zone, you will begin to experience the growth and freedom that are waiting for you.

Today, I challenge you to open yourself up to life's pruning process. Identify at least one thing you need to let go of, and take the first step to unclench it from your grasp. (Do it *now*—don't wait and second-guess yourself, or you'll never do it.) I promise, you'll be happy you did!

New beginnings can be scary. You cannot always plan how things will turn out. Choose to let your faith be stronger than your fear.

# Change of Plans

"I'll be happy when . . ." We've all thought this at some point in our lives. Feeling as though our happiness lies somewhere outside of where we are and that our contentment is wrapped up inside the next promotion we get, the next milestone we reach, or the next title added to our names. It's called Destination Addiction, and it can steal your joy if you let it.

After the car accident, when my doctors told me it would be years before it was safe for me to have another baby, I remember how crushed I felt. All the medications I was on would take time to heal my body and brain, and then I'd have to allow time for them to clear out of my system completely before trying to conceive. My daughter, Bean, was three years old at the time, and when I got the news, I was just starting to believe I could handle caring for another tiny human. I was devastated. Bean had been begging for a sibling, and I was excited about them being close enough in age to be playmates. But life had other plans.

Now, every time I see Bean and Dom together, my heart melts. Even with a seven-year age difference, their obsession with each other is undeniable. Bean is the perfect big sister: protective, nurturing, and always ready to help—with the exception of diaper-changing time, of course.

Life didn't happen as I had planned, but it is more beautiful than I could have ever imagined. What in your life has turned out differently than you expected? Treasure the little nuggets of hope that may not come when you planned them but seem to appear at just the right time.

Trust the timing of your life even if it's happening differently than you hoped or expected.

# Be Authentic

My biggest fear growing up was that I would have a birthday party and no one would show up. I'm not sure where that fear originated—or why the thought still causes me incredible discomfort.

Friendships have always been a little tricky for me. Growing up in small-town Louisiana, I attended school in an environment where most people did not look like me. I never felt like I fit in. I did my best to conform. To observe. To learn everything I could about the dos and don'ts. To make sure who I was didn't make anyone around me uncomfortable.

The person I presented to the world was palatable and easygoing, someone who avoided confrontation and difficult conversations at all costs. I felt I couldn't be fully myself because that might single me out even more than I already felt I was. I just wanted to blend into the background: *Nobody look at me, or notice me, or make a big deal that I'm here. I'll be quiet and behave. If I don't draw attention to myself, you won't even know I'm here.*

Once I was out on my own, living life and learning about myself, I simply refused to be anything other than exactly who I was. *This is me. Take it or leave it.* And I found myself with a core friend group consisting of about three to four people. Quality over quantity.

Do you have quality people? People you can be honest with? Ugly cry with? Pray with? Have fun with? People you can trust to show up for you with the same love and dedication that you show to them?

Being myself relieves me of the pressure of performing. It releases me from the responsibility of managing people's perceptions of me. It can be so liberating. It can do the same for you!

# Address Difficulties

Who hates conflict? I do, I do!

On any conflict styles assessment, I am always smack-dab in the middle of "accommodator" and "avoider." If I could go through life without ever having to address anything uncomfortable with anyone, I'd be a happy woman.

Maybe you can relate.

A situation happens with a family member or close friend. You don't like the way she treated you or spoke to you, but maybe you misinterpreted her actions. *She's a nice person and probably didn't mean for it to come off that way. Maybe she was just having a bad day. I'd be stressed out too if I had her kids. Bless her heart. If it were me, I'd want someone to be understanding, so I should give her grace too. It's the right thing to do.* You decide to let it go.

But you *can't* just let it go, can you? You find yourself either avoiding her or walking on eggshells around her. You know you need to say something, but the thought of doing so is terrifying. You're so anxious that you've been grinding your teeth without realizing it, so now you've got a headache that won't go away. Meanwhile she's been floating along, blissfully unaware that you're on the verge of a stomach ulcer and your head feels like it's about to explode.

Perhaps you're afraid to offend someone by addressing an issue, or you're sacrificing your physical and mental health to keep the peace. You do not have to neglect your feelings to preserve someone else's. Your feelings matter. It's not your responsibility to harbor discomfort in order to keep others comfortable. You can be who you are and handle the situation in a way that isn't inappropriate or unnecessarily confrontational.

Sometimes self-care requires you to have difficult conversations with people you love. You are capable of addressing tough situations with compassion and care.

# Prioritize Peace

I once attended a silent retreat in a beautiful, rural community right outside of Atlanta. The breathtaking views immediately brought peace to my mind and body. To get eight full hours of silence on top of that was just icing on the cake! My introverted heart was doing cartwheels in my chest! What an *absolute* dream!

I spent the entire day focused on wellness: walking the labyrinth, meditating, journaling, deep breathing, and observing nature. I felt so calm, relaxed, and fulfilled. The nagging anxiety I usually experience was nonexistent. My mind was clear. My body felt lighter.

As the day came to an end, I realized I would have to leave this sacred space and return to my "normal" life, where I could not control the sensory input and noise levels that overstimulated me every day. *How do I preserve my peace when others enter my environment? How do I maintain a sense of calm when I have to interact with other people? Is it even possible?* Instead of giving in to panic, I took some deep breaths and allowed myself to consider that peace is possible. That was the first step—acknowledging that peace is available to me.

The key to prioritizing peace is to be intentional about having peace within you, even when chaos swirls all around you. How do you do that? You concentrate on your breath. You place your hand over your heart, and close your eyes. You think calming thoughts. You become the epicenter of the stillness you desire.

Make peace a priority. Peace is grounding. Whenever possible, separate yourself from people and situations that withdraw more than they deposit into you. Speak positive words over yourself and repeat them often. Believe you can maintain the peace that supports your mental health and well-being.

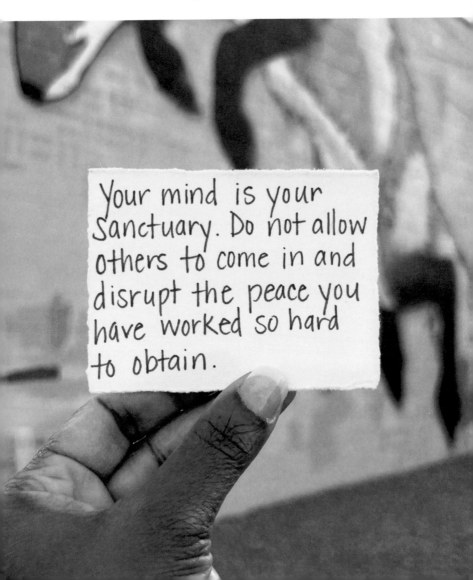

# Change Direction

It's amazing to me that change is one of the most inevitable elements of life, and yet it is one of the things we resist the most. To many of us, *change* is a dirty word that is better left unsaid. Because change requires something of us. It requires us to take action. It requires us to do something differently than we've always done it. It not only requires movement, but movement in a direction that may be wholly unfamiliar or uncomfortable or downright frightening to us.

So we attempt to avoid change. Even when we know the path we're on isn't leading us where we're destined to be. Not only is it not leading us there; sometimes it leads us so far away from where we need to be that when we stop and look around, we don't even recognize where we are, much less remember how we got here.

Change makes us afraid. We're afraid of messing up. We're afraid of what others might think about us. We're afraid we don't have what it takes to succeed. We're afraid of the variables we can't control. We're afraid we may regret our choice.

I don't know about you, but I'd rather put in the work, jump off the cliff, and trust that my parachute opens before I hit the ground, rather than spend the rest of my life wondering what kind of impact I could have made on the world if only I'd had the courage to get out of my own way.

Don't let fear win. You have the courage and authority within you. Changing your direction could change your life.

If what you've been doing isn't working any more, choose to shift into a nother direction. You have the authority to change the trajectory of your life.

# Nurture Your Light

Your light is your truth. It is the essence of who you are. It distinguishes you from the darkness of the world around you. Wherever you go, your light precedes you. Although it is beautiful and illuminating, your light can also be an irritant to some.

For years, that concept puzzled me. Why are my kindness and optimism so bothersome to some people? Is there something wrong with me? Do I not seem genuine?

I wondered if perhaps those people had encountered more darkness than light in their lives. Maybe they had not experienced authentic compassion, causing them to be skeptical of any sympathy offered to them. Whatever the reason, I cannot change who I am to ease their discomfort. I have to be true to who I am.

I began sharing my story, and in doing so transparently, I shifted my identity from victim to victor. More than anything, I want to help others see that they have everything they need inside them to do the same, that empathy and love can help bring light to even the darkest spaces and seasons of our lives. Having the courage to pursue my personal healing created a platform for mental health and wellness I never dreamed possible. Someone out there is in desperate need of the glow that radiates from me. I will not be less of who I am or allow the perceptions of others to dictate how brightly my light shines.

Is this a challenge for you? Has there ever been a situation in your life when you felt compelled to show up as less than your true self to keep the peace or avoid offending someone?

Will you allow others to dim your light or, worse, convince you to keep it from shining at all? Be true to yourself. Nurture your light and change the world.

# Embrace Discomfort

I have an aversion to discomfort. For me, discomfort implies change, uncertainty, and ultimately, risk. I prefer to plan and be prepared for things. Life, however, seems not to care about my desire for stability and likes to throw things my way that burn all my little color-coded plans to the ground. If everything going on in the world right now disturbs your spirit and mind and soul, embrace that feeling. That discomfort, that uneasiness, serves a purpose.

Yeah, I know it sounds outlandish. Many of us spend a significant amount of time trying to avoid discomfort at all costs. We look for the easiest, most convenient way to accomplish a task. We do our best to dodge uncomfortable situations or difficult conversations we need to have with others. We like to pretend that everything is the same as it was, and we can continue with business as usual.

Without discomfort, we feel no motivation to shift. Discomfort, however, is a sign that something needs to grow or change. Ninety-nine percent of the time, that something is us.

When we are comfortable, we become complacent, and we feel no sense of urgency to take action. We don't lean into those disagreeable feelings and ask ourselves the difficult questions. We don't step out of our comfort zones or try new things.

*Today*, make the commitment to yourself and your community to stop planning and start doing. Stop contemplating *all the things* and start doing at least *one thing*. Take the first step, and then the next best step, and then the next. When we work together in love and compassion and kindness, we ignite the inner power we all possess to change the world.

Embrace discomfort. In the process of struggle, real transformation happens.

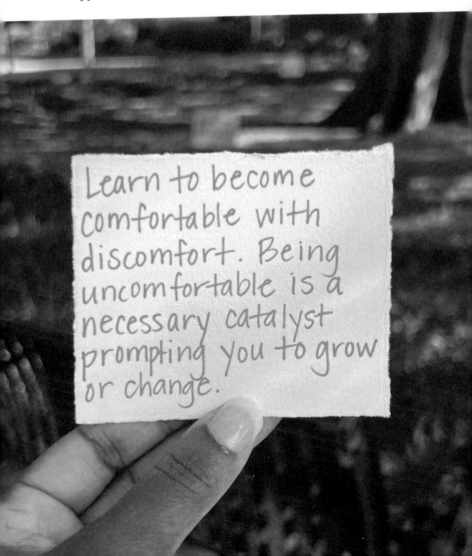

Learn to become comfortable with discomfort. Being uncomfortable is a necessary catalyst prompting you to grow or change.

# Trust Your Intuition

Maybe we don't trust ourselves. Maybe we were never encouraged to be independent thinkers. Maybe we were conditioned to believe that we couldn't trust our own voice. That we would make a mistake and cause irreparable damage to our lives. We were silenced as children and teenagers, and then we were expected to magically speak up for ourselves as adults.

But how can we suddenly do that when we weren't taught to advocate for ourselves? Someone else always did it for us. Someone else told us what choice to make. They told us what to do and when to do it. So now, when we have to make a decision, we freeze. Panic sets in and paralyzes us. We feel unprepared and unequipped to make a sound choice. We are afraid that we are not qualified to make decisions that are best for us.

I was terrified to start my own business. With everything going on in my life, most people told me to wait and just focus on my recovery. But I trusted my gut and did it gradually, at a pace I could sustain. It was one of the best decisions I have ever made.

You can learn to trust your intuition, inner knowing, intelligence, and ability to make well-informed decisions. It will take some time to adjust your way of thinking. You will have to speak encouraging words to yourself. You will have to push through the skepticism and reluctance. You will have to learn to distinguish between your voice and the voices that have taken precedence in your mind. But you can do it.

That "feeling" you have about that man, that friend, that job, that babysitter, that business partner, that classmate your child wants to meet at the movies—is your intuition.

You can trust yourself rather than deferring to someone else who assumes they know what's best for you.

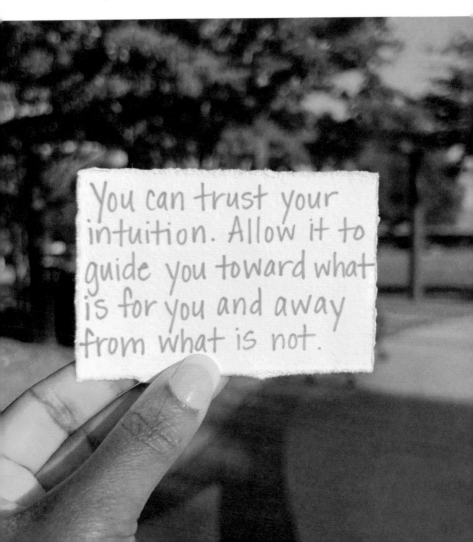

You can trust your intuition. Allow it to guide you toward what is for you and away from what is not.

# Bloom Unapologetically

I have often thought to myself:

*I'm just shy. I've always been that way.*

*I've always been quiet.*

*I don't like drawing attention to myself.*

*I'm more of a background person.*

*I don't like people looking at me.*

*Being around new people makes me anxious.*

Do you think things like that? Is that your truth? Or is that what you've been conditioned to think about yourself? Have you been manipulated into loneliness?

Maybe someone told you that you were too much—too loud, too needy, too attention-seeking, too energetic, too headstrong, too strong-willed. So you learned to shrink. To make yourself smaller, to whittle your personality down into tiny, digestible chunks that the people around you could handle. That they could be comfortable with. That didn't challenge them or their preconceived notions and assumptions. Or make them take a closer look at themselves.

You took on the role they told you was best for your personality. But it was probably most convenient for them. Until now, you've forced yourself to be content with that role. But as you grow and change and heal and peel back some of those layers, the role you've been playing may not cut it anymore. Maybe you want to step out more. Try new things. Showcase your talents and allow them to be noticed. You are ready to feel that sense of satisfaction and fulfillment from stretching beyond your comfort zone.

Give that version of yourself a chance. Allow her voice to be heard. Let her advocate for herself. Listen to her ideas. Consider her suggestions. Accept her uniqueness.

Embrace her. Make her feel welcome. Let her know that you appreciate her and you're so glad to see her come out of her shell. Let her bloom.

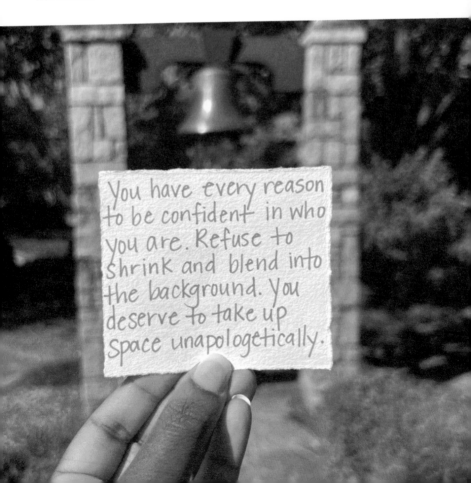

## DAY 86

# Overcome Challenges

Without exerting any effort at all, I could rattle off the many ways my days are challenging. Managing the residual repercussions and side effects of a traumatic brain injury are difficult. More often than not:

- I don't feel motivated.
- The things that others do easily, quickly, or efficiently seem like scaling Mount Everest to me.
- I am overstimulated by the sensory input around me.
- I question my ability to continue to do this work.
- I worry that if people knew how challenging it was for me to be productive every day, they would discredit the things I try so hard to accomplish.

It's tempting to give up. To abandon hope. To wonder if what I'm doing even matters enough to justify the sacrifice. If I feel most days like I'm surviving rather than thriving, am I really *living* life? I just want things not to be so hard.

But even when I'm in the trenches of self-doubt and uncertainty, my tenacious brain is up there fighting, saying things like:

*Yep, I know this is hard, but I have this new affirmation I need to write down before I forget it. Bean and Dom are so sweet to each other. My husband is making my favorite turkey burgers for dinner. One of my counseling clients is close to a breakthrough. That dress I'm planning to wear today looks incredible on me. And that new Fenty concealer I bought makes me look fresh-faced and well rested.*

I know it's difficult. I know people don't get it; they can't possibly understand what you go through every day just to show up. And even though it's hard, you are doing an amazing job. You haven't given up. You overcome challenges every single day. You have the courage to try even when you know it won't be easy. *That's* what matters.

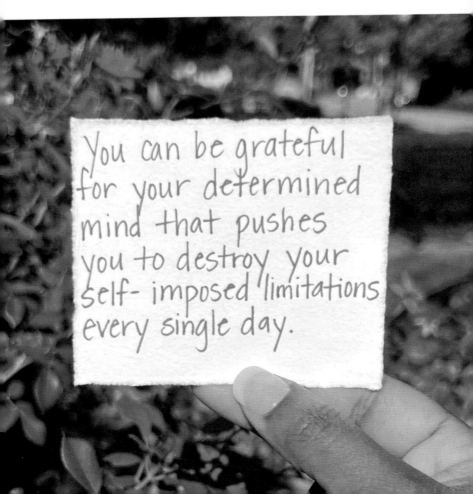

You can be grateful for your determined mind that pushes you to destroy your self-imposed limitations every single day.

# Commitment

*You are worth the commitment it takes to heal. You are not broken, and you do not need to be fixed. There are parts of you that have been wounded and need to be rehabilitated. You deserve to invest in yourself, whatever it takes, to get to the healthy space you desire.*

These are words I have repeated to myself many, many times.

Full transparency: in the beginning of the healing process, you may feel more hurt than you do inside the dysfunction you're walking away from. Because dysfunction can be loyal company. You know it's not good for you, but it's sufficient for now, and it doesn't require you to uproot your life.

More than likely, when you start your healing journey, you're going to experience some resistance. You'll come up with a million reasons why that stagnant space you're in really isn't *that bad*. But ultimately the choice is yours to make: commit or be complacent. Are you willing to do the hard work it takes to redirect the trajectory of your life? To reject the notion that you're *supposed* to be at least a little bit miserable and construct a new normal for yourself? To accept that being overjoyed and euphoric is not some unrealistic expectation or fantasy? You can allow yourself to feel these emotions without being skeptical of them.

We all experience hurts, struggles, and personal traumas. Sometimes we feel debilitating guilt when we try to prioritize ourselves and practice self-care. We all want to know that someone cares about us. Even if no one else does, care for yourself. Commit to living your life with joy and intention, even when the process feels uncomfortable. Do it regardless of what anyone else thinks. You are worth it.

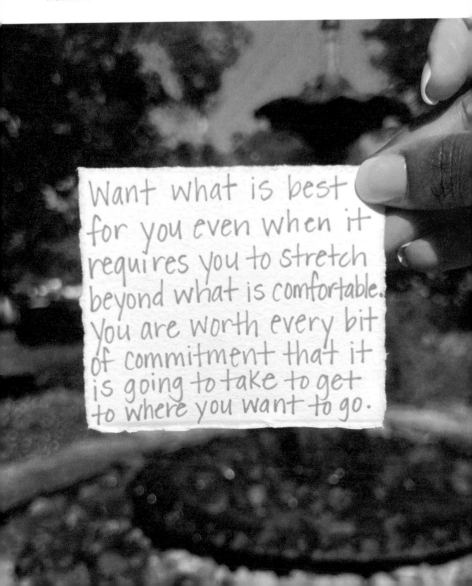

Want what is best for you even when it requires you to stretch beyond what is comfortable. You are worth every bit of commitment that it is going to take to get to where you want to go.

# One Step at a Time

Your calling won't always feel comfortable for you. Most times, what you're called to do will stretch you and push you to grow far beyond what you ever thought was possible. Writing a book definitely stretched me!

Maybe you don't have a degree in it.

You have zero experience.

It's the exact opposite of what people told you that you were good at as a kid.

It's something you never saw yourself doing or wanting to do ever before.

Or it's something you've always wanted to do, but at some point you were discouraged or criticized, and so you did what you thought was the right thing and made the safe choice.

But for many of us, that thing we're meant to do just will not leave us alone. It's no coincidence the world has been dropping little hints everywhere you turn. You feel in your soul that you have this incredible idea for a book, and out of nowhere, a literary agent contacts you. For years, you've wanted to start an after-school enrichment program for the youth in your community, and you get a random email with a list of available grants to fund the program.

The fear inside you or the fearful people around you may tell you what you want to do is too big. It'll be too hard and take too much work. In those moments, allow your faith to be stronger than your fear. Your faith knows you may not always do it perfectly. You may stumble along the way. You may have to backtrack and do some things differently. But you will give your best effort regardless.

So on the days when things seem impossible, remember, sweet friend: One step at a time. One breath at a time. You can do this.

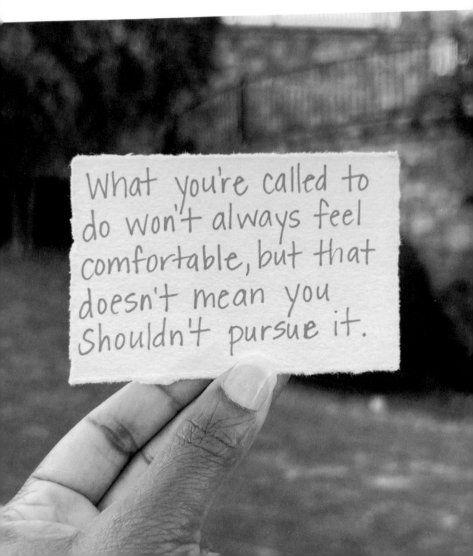

# Life Is Hard

When I look back over the last few years, my heart is full of gratitude. Without a doubt, 2018 was the *hardest* year of my life, and it is a miracle that I made it through in one piece. There were days when my body felt broken, my soul was weary, and I didn't want to get out of bed. I didn't want to write one of those encouraging notes. I didn't want to show up for myself, much less anyone else.

Living with a traumatic brain injury is *hard*.

Going three to four days without sleeping on a regular basis is *hard*.

Having migraines so mind-numbing and intense that you can barely see, and being terrified that if you go to sleep you might not wake up is *hard*.

Encouraging others when you feel like falling apart is *hard*.

Trying to be somebody's wife and somebody's mama when you're not quite sure who *you* are anymore is *hard*.

Many days, it takes every ounce of everything I have to show up. But I will *always* show up. There is no other choice. Because I'm learning to use hard things to become stronger. Because someone else needs to see that they can show up too. Even when it's hard. Especially when it's hard.

Because no matter what, we can and we will do lots of hard things.

This is for *you*. The person who's thinking about giving up because healing might hurt too much. Who's considering hiding your battle scars because folks won't "get it." Who's decided that nobody would even notice or care if you never got out of bed again. I see you. I feel you. I've been there. Heck, some days I'm still there. But you can do this. You will do this! And it will be so worth it.

Today accept that you are no longer the person you once were. Give yourself permission to pause, to rest, to heal, and to evolve. Love and embrace the person you're becoming.

# Open Your Heart

If we live long enough, we will all experience some form of disappointment, betrayal, or heartbreak. And it will hurt. Tears may flow. We might take up kickboxing to diffuse some of the anger. We may get a makeover, go on a shopping spree, or take a trip to distract ourselves from the pain we feel.

If you're like me, you may have experienced a level of anguish and despair from which you never thought you'd recover. Maybe life has dealt you such a devastating blow. Perhaps you thought you'd never be able to love again. To forgive. To open your heart and be vulnerable, when you could just as easily build a brick wall around your heart, with barbed wire at the top for good measure.

You cannot live anything other than your truth. Do not give up on love, friendship, companionship. Allow healing to flow through you and repair the wounds on your heart. Listen to your inner knowing so that you don't project the shortcomings of a select few onto the rest of the people in your life or ones you may meet in the future.

The part of you that craves connection and intimacy with others will help you hold on to the belief that your people are out there. People who will love and accept you exactly as you are. Who will have your back. Who will not take advantage of the space you allow them to occupy in your life. Who will treasure being in relationship with you and feel blessed to do life with you. Hold on to that part of yourself. Breathe. Forgive. Open your heart to love.

# About the Author

Faith Broussard Cade gained a large Instagram following when she started posting daily handwritten positive affirmations (or "love notes") on her account @fleurdelisspeaks. What started as a fifteen-day self-love challenge as she grappled with recovering from a traumatic brain injury has grown into a loyal following and an uplifting community supporting mental health, wellness, and love. Faith serves private clients as a mental health counselor and coach but also uses her experience and expertise to solve accessibility problems for her community. The former school counselor now shares content about mental health and her personal healing journey to inspire women to prioritize peace, boundaries, and emotional well-being in their lives and relationships. She lives with her husband and two children in Atlanta, Georgia.

*From the Publisher*

# GREAT BOOKS
## ARE EVEN BETTER WHEN THEY'RE SHARED!

### Help other readers find this one:

- Post a review at your favorite online bookseller

- Post a picture on a social media account and share why you enjoyed it

- Send a note to a friend who would also love it—or better yet, give them a copy

*Thanks for reading!*